C000053974

Elvis & Buddy
Linked Lives

Elvis & Buddy
Linked Lives

Alan Mann

MUSIC MENTOR BOOKS
York, England

© 2002 Alan Mann. All rights reserved. First edition.
United States Copyright Registration applied for.

The right of Alan Mann to be identified as Author of this Work has been asserted in accordance with the UK *Copyright, Designs and Patents Act 1988.*

Every effort has been made to trace the copyright holders of material used in this volume. Should there be any omissions in this respect, we apologise and shall be pleased to make the appropriate acknowledgments in future printings.

A full list of illustrations and photo credits appears on page 158. The trade mark 'Brunswick' appears by kind permission of the owners.

All rights reserved. No part of this publication may be reproduced, stored in a retrieval system or transmitted in any form by any means, electronic, mechanical, reprographic, recording or otherwise without prior written permission from the publisher.

This book is sold subject to the conditions that it shall not, by way of trade or otherwise, be lent, resold, hired out or otherwise circulated without the publisher's prior consent in any form of binding or cover other than that in which it is published and without a similar condition including this condition being imposed on the subsequent purchaser.

Whilst every effort has been made to ensure the correctness of information included in this book, the publisher makes no representation — either express or implied — as to its accuracy and cannot accept any legal responsibility for any errors or omissions or consequences arising therefrom.

British Library Cataloguing-in-Publication Data
A catalogue record for this book is available from the British Library.

ISBN 0 9519888 5 9

Front cover illustration by Simon Pritchard.

Published worldwide by Music Mentor Books *(Proprietor: G.R. Groom-White)*
69 Station Road, Upper Poppleton, York YO26 6PZ, North Yorkshire, England.
Telephone/Fax: +44 (0)1904 330308   *email:* music.mentor@lineone.net

Technical support by PJP Information Systems, Bradford, West Yorkshire.

Cover by Raven Design, Ware, Hertfordshire.

Printed and bound in Great Britain by Antony Rowe Ltd, Chippenham, Wiltshire.

Personal Prologue

The framework of this book already existed a couple of years ago, as did one linking the lives of Gene Vincent and Eddie Cochran which had to be sidelined. As a fan of Fifties music, I had begun to feel more and more as the years went by that the music hadn't just happened by accident and maybe there was a deeper strand. Initially, I simply planned to juxtapose the career of each man while maybe adding a little food for thought along the way. The idea was that this would allow me to develop the inner core of the work which would dwell on how and why the singers came to meet up at all in 1955 and the significance, if any, of those meetings.

Originally there wasn't going to be any 'paranormal' content until one rainy day whilst in a holiday cottage I chanced upon some reading material left by the owners and began browsing in a desultory way through a large book on horoscopes while waiting for the weather to brighten. The reader must believe me when I say that astrology is not a subject I'm familiar with outside of occasionally glancing at my daily star sign in the newspaper and giving out the odd chuckle. I am not a convert and, where matters of a superstitious nature are involved, I'd be quite happy to walk under a ladder — although perhaps on reflection better not make that on Friday the 13th!

The bulky book that started me wondering was called *The Secret Language of Relationships*, which provided a profile under various days of the calendar year and one was invited to look up one's own birth date in conjunction with that of a husband/wife or partner and read the comments. The aim was to answer the question as to what would happen when any two individuals came together and their energies combined. Perhaps to live happily ever after, or perhaps to have a highly volatile relationship. Quite a detailed prognosis was given for over a thousand such conjunctions.

Having discovered that my wife and I (Scorpio and Taurus) are quite firmly linked together, I decided for fun to look at the conjunction of Elvis Presley and Buddy Holly, not expecting anything other than fairly bland comments. After all, I was simply putting two birth dates together; the identities of the dead singers were not an integral part of the equation. However, I do recall hoping that the entry wouldn't be too upbeat given that the life of each man had been cut tragically short. Imagine my surprise when they were described as symbiotic peas in a pod bound together by a fatal karmic twist! These two individuals (whoever they might be and anonymous as far as the book was concerned) were strongly linked together for better or for worse — much more dramatically than most other pairings it seemed! Such portentous vibes got me thinking.

Whilst all of this was in no way proof positive, it really did focus my mind on the lives of these two great artists with the added thought that maybe it was not pure chance that pulled them towards one another like iron filings being drawn by a magnet. Perhaps the oft-expressed thought that there is nothing in this world that is down to chance alone is actually true, and neither are there such things as pure coincidences?

It can probably be seen already from these brief opening words that the spiritual dimension of the two singers' lives will indeed be touched upon, although hopefully not in a way the reader will find either wacky or flippant. But neither will we be solemn, and one thing you can be sure of is that there will be no claims that Elvis — or Buddy Holly for that matter — is alive and well but in hiding, or waiting to be cloned. Certainly, neither man was the victim of any sort of conspiracy and no such propositions will be championed here.

It seems to me that each lived out their allotted time-span, and that gives us much interesting, down-to-earth stuff to chew over in the music and the careers of both for starters. To leaven the necessary biographical content somewhat, I've punctuated the space between chapters with '*Musical Interludes*'. In these, we'll link together and take a closer look at various recordings our subjects made, the hope being that this will give additional insight into precisely what made them tick.

What is particularly interesting to reflect on — and is the original *raison d'être* for this book — is that Elvis and Buddy *did* get to meet in their earliest days, and what went on when they did is definitely worth investigating and in some detail. After that, we'll see where all of this leads us.

Alan Mann

Acknowledgments

The main people I wish to include here are those of my family and immediate circle of friends who didn't seek to ostracise me when I announced my intention of writing this book, even if a quizzical eyebrow or two was raised. My son Richard championed the book at every stage, as did my wife Pam and daughters Karen and Nicola. The other main inspirations without whom this wouldn't have been possible are the redoubtable 'Johns' of the Buddy Holly world — Messrs. Ingman and Beecher — who continue to promote the music at every opportunity. In particular, it was the former who kindly vetted the chapter on 1955, putting me right on many important occasions and whom I must single out. However, I must also assure readers that any errors which remain are solely my responsibility.

I've had a small but vital amount of musical input from Crickets Jerry Allison and Sonny Curtis in Tennessee, who were in Lubbock circa 1955 and remember those days with great affection. Trevor Cajiao (editor of *Now Dig This* and *Elvis — The Man And His Music*) was particularly helpful on the Presley side of things, whilst the two hundred-odd copies of that bible of rock & roll, *Now Dig This*, in my possession were a goldmine of information of all sorts. Jim Carr, editor of the *Holly International* magazine, was similarly helpful on the Holly side of the divide. Knowledgeable fans of many years standing aren't forgotten either, such as Paul and Dot King, Peter Feast, Ian Higham, Wayne Smith, Goff Pattinson, Clive Harvey, Chris Rees and Tina, Trevor Hardy, Ian Westgate, Steve Cairns, Bob Watson, John Firminger (*Crickets File*) and, from the *Out Of Time* record shop in Norwich, the redoubtable Eric White (all in England). Bob Dees, Howard Olson and Shawn Nagy of Prairie Dog from the USA, and the Australian posse of Damian Johnstone, Nigel Smith and Jim Boot are all owed a special 'thank you' for their unconditional support.

A recent friend is the Canadian entertainer Johnny Vallis, who exhibits a deep love of the music whilst still being relatively young in years, and kindly supplied the army photo of Elvis with Buddy Knox. Almost last, but certainly not least, are the former Big Beats drummer Jerry Zapata and his wife Kathy in Las Vegas. Jerry had the enviable pleasure of having met both Elvis ('the most beautiful human being I ever saw') and Buddy Holly during his time as a musician, and not too many of us can say that. Local artist and friend Simon Pritchard supplied the excellent front cover artwork and I'm grateful for all his support, not forgetting his partner and true Buddy Holly devotee, Susie. My deep apologies to any others who ought to have a name check but are assuredly the victims of one of many 'senior moments' by the author. I hope they will forgive the oversight and accept this blanket thanks.

Of course, anyone who writes a book and mentions Buddy Holly cannot do so without acknowledging the pioneering work done over the years by many individuals such as Bill Griggs, John Goldrosen and (once again)

John Beecher and many others whose works have been heavily consulted, as the *Bibliography* will attest. In contrast, the life of Elvis was more heavily documented from the outset, although it is only in recent years that it has been possible to get a real insight and overview of his life and times. We all need each other's help, and the thought must be that no one individual has sole trusteeship of the memory of either Elvis Presley or of Buddy Holly. Remember that we're all just passing through.

A heartfelt note of thanks is also due to the astrologer Christine Leveridge. Faced with my most unusual request to investigate and contrast the birth charts of both singers, she not only did so with enthusiasm but produced a veritable torrent of observations, data and comments for me to ponder.

I must give a particularly warm thank you to George White of Music Mentor Books, who not only agreed to publish this work but has shown great enthusiasm for the project from the moment he was first approached. He went on to give generously of his time and expertise at every point along the way, and has truly become my own trusty 'music mentor' for the final twelve months or so that this book has taken to come to print.

Finally, in the tradition that the last shall be first and the first last, this book is dedicated with love to my wife Pam, who has lived through the lengthy gestation period of this book with infinite fortitude and cheerful good humour well beyond the course of duty. I know too, that she will not mind sharing this dedication with the name of my late father, Salem John Mann, who passed away in 2001 when nearing the end of his 98th year. He's missed far more than he could ever begin to realise.

Contents

Contents

Introduction

They say that in life only two things are certain (that's surely obvious, death and rock & roll — what else?) but maybe there could be another contender as we enter the Twenty-First Century, and that is that simply far too many books have been written about Elvis Presley — and some not always for the soundest of reasons! An incontrovertible if somewhat frivolous thought. At first glance, perhaps the present book itself fits neatly into such a category? Certainly, if the sole content were only those brief early meetings of Buddy Holly and Elvis Presley, then any resulting manuscript would indeed end up a pretty slim if fascinating affair. Having said that, a lengthy book was written a few years back about Presley's one fleeting meeting with the Beatles, so there is a precedent! However, let us make our own case.

It is widely known that both men had enthralling careers prematurely curtailed by tragic endings, so examining their lives and music in tandem can be of profound interest given that a perspective of nearly fifty years is now involved and so much research has been undertaken over the years for us to utilise. Some of this information can be threaded together and connects these two musical icons in a variety of ways. The links involved actual physical meetings in 1955, but were rather more metaphysical in nature in the years before and after.

It has, in fact, been a particular fascination of the author for years that Elvis and Buddy 'ran around together' in Lubbock, Texas during 1955, before either had made their mark on the national scene. Now, for the first time ever, in-depth information is given of all those meetings, and it is that which forms the inner core of the book and which sparks off several lines of discussion to lead us in some surprising directions. That these musical shooting stars came together in that year, spun around each other virtually unnoticed, then flew off in different directions to make such indelible marks on the popular musical firmament is undeniable. Even if we can't time-travel, our fortunate Twenty-First Century viewpoint can bring us rich rewards in such delvings and justifiably add a further ingredient to the legend and mystique that continues to surround both Elvis Aaron Presley (1935–77) and Charles Hardin Holley* (1936–59).

There is a particularly interesting caveat to the foregoing which can't be avoided and needs to be mentioned right at the outset: namely, that a 1959 letter attributed to Elvis Presley came to light a few years ago which includes the intriguing phrase '*I'd never met Buddy Holly personally*'! However, please don't stop reading quite yet, because this surprising and erroneous statement (sorry to correct you, Elvis) plus the contents of the letter and how it came to be written are fully discussed in a later chapter. For meet they most certainly did on several occasions, and we'll remind Elvis of

---

* Although he didn't change it until 1956, Buddy's surname is spelt 'Holly' throughout the book to avoid confusion.

those times with a wealth of overwhelming detail thrown in for good measure.

But first we have to set the scene, which will also give us a useful insight into some of the major ingredients that led to the birth of rock & roll mid-way through the path of the last century.

- CHAPTER 1 -

Have You Heard The News?

Music, the post-war elixir

An occasional daydream of the author is to imagine being a spectator or a fly on the wall at some other point in time or place, and preferably well away from the constraints of one's present humdrum existence. For example, a criminologist from the last century might contemplate being in or around Dealey Plaza in Dallas on 22 November 1963 to see if he could spot the glint of a protruding rifle from a nondescript book depository as a presidential motorcade approached, whilst a journalist in earlier times might even wish to lurk on a deck of the *Titanic* if a seat in a lifeboat could be guaranteed and a waterproof notebook were part of his baggage. This scribe, however, would choose a seemingly much more humble and unlikely venue, though it would certainly be no less fascinating to those with an ear for musical history.

Yours truly would have chosen to be in Lubbock, Texas during 1955 at either the Cotton Club or the nearby Fair Park Coliseum to witness a young Buddy Holly come face to face with his new idol, Elvis Presley, and to listen to the conversations that went back and forth between them. Mostly about music, but Texan girls would undoubtedly have also got the occasional mention! Neither man had found fame or fortune at that time, although Elvis was just beginning to raise up a Southern storm that within the short space of a few years would encircle the entire globe. By that time, his young friend would be lying in a quiet Lubbock cemetery, his life over and his brief musical journey cut short but in some ways surprisingly complete. Their lives would never again intermingle so tangibly but, juxtaposed, they make for some fascinating reflection and analysis as the following pages will reveal.

In fact, it was on Thursday, 6 January 1955 that the eighteen year old Buddy first went along to a packed Fair Park Coliseum in Lubbock to watch a country bill featuring the nineteen year old sensation, Elvis Presley (he'd turn twenty that same week). Life for the bespectacled young wannabe from Texas — who hadn't yet donned the heavy horn-rims that later became his trademark — and for many other youngsters in the audience was never to be quite the same again.

There is no doubt that the appearance of Elvis Presley on the scene during the previous year had let the genie out of the bottle for both musicians and fans alike — even if the older generation continued to try and hold back the incoming musical tide that threatened to engulf America. It would come to influence not just popular music but virtually every aspect of mass culture, and along the way introduce a new expression — or rather *phenomenon* — of

13

'teenagers' into public consciousness.

Remember — if you need reminding — that the year 1955 when Buddy and Elvis first crossed paths was far back in time, and life then was markedly different from today in virtually every conceivable way.

In the United States of America where our tale unfolds, Dwight D. Eisenhower, an austere former Army General, had held the presidential reins since 1953 as the drama of the Second World War was finally fading almost a decade since peace was formalised. The impact of the conflict, which had engulfed virtually the whole of the civilised world, would continue to reverberate throughout the remainder of that century. Loudly at first, then as a backdrop while life gradually got back to some sort of normality, with the determination for most that this would mean discarding the Thirties and the years that followed: a period of intense anxiety and economic depression culminating in the eventual outbreak of a second World War less than twenty years after the ending of the war to supposedly end all wars.

In the gradually reviving United States, the No. 1 record as 1955 got underway was a powerful ballad, *Let Me Go, Lover* by eighteen year old Joan Weber, one of many white balladeers of the day who it seemed really might rule the hit parade for years to come. Back then, only a handful of non-white artists such as Billy Eckstine, the Cuban-born bandleader Perez Prado and the blind ballad singer Al Hibbler ever got near to the main charts which still carried with them the whiff of past segregation. Recordings by black artists invariably ended up in the more obscure R&B charts, which were far from mainstream at that point.

The 'rock history' time-clock had hardly started ticking as such — in fact, the term didn't even exist then, but was a phenomenon still waiting to be identified and labelled. However, once the phrase was coined, it would lead to the music being analysed and dissected *ad nauseam* over the years at rates that show little sign of abating. But whether one should take such proliferating musical scribes too seriously is a moot point. Perhaps instead we should reflect on the old adage that no-one ever erects statues to critics!

Over in the UK meanwhile, we were still listening to a mixture of British and Transatlantic artists like Vera Lynn, Doris Day, Slim Whitman and the novelty whistler Ronnie Ronalde. If there was any musical beat — syncopated or otherwise — reaching our sheltered ears over here, we had to strain to find it. Unless you were able to tune in to the American Forces Network, the highlights were probably the weekly *Billy Cotton Band Show* on the BBC Light Programme, the English broadcasts on Radio Luxembourg, and — for those lucky enough to live within travelling distance of a theatre — the occasional personal appearances of that flamboyant early visitor, the so-called 'Nabob Of Sob', Johnnie Ray.

---

* Based on an original composition by Jenny Lou Carson called *Let Me Go, Devil* — an Alcoholics Anonymous-slanted pitch against the demon rum — the song was deftly rewritten by Columbia staffer Al Hill into a steamy romantic million-seller for Weber. Her record shot into the charts after six excerpts from it were featured in a televison drama called *Studio One*, resulting in 500,000 orders within a fortnight. Although she eventually turned out to be a one-hit wonder, Joan Weber was the first artist to get a record into the hit parade as a direct result of TV promotion. It was the beginning of a new era.

14

Ray's amazing run of twenty-one UK hits had reached its first peak in 1954 when the highly risqué *Such A Night*[*] made the No. 1 spot. Although Britain was enjoying the balm of peace, with major post-war reconstruction coming to an end, the musical scene was in a deepening trough that would eventually lead to a shake-up of a seismic nature. Although we didn't know it then, the seeds for this were already being sown over in the United States and way down below the Mason-Dixon Line with a certain young Elvis Presley playing a leading role.

Looking back from our vantage point and using the lives of Elvis Presley and Buddy Holly as a backdrop, let's try our best to briefly re-enter the Fifties, even as they are receding and becoming a distant and increasingly bygone age. It was the literary giant Arthur Koestler who said that, in peering into the past you can analyse the ashes but can't resurrect the flames. Well, maybe not, but certainly nobody suggests we can't try.

To reconstruct those meetings between Elvis and Buddy won't be very easy, but the result should be well worth it. The Fifties were a magical period if you lived through them and retain the rose-tinted specs (or even those 3-D ones that you were occasionally handed as you walked into the local cinema). Certainly, it is an era that has deeply touched other generations as nostalgia envelops and the good is selectively remembered, while the not-so-good — of which the Fifties certainly had its ample quota — is mercifully edited out of our collective memories.

However, before we get to focus on 1955 itself, there's lots to talk about, so to set the scene let us first take a brief look at each of the main men in our story — for, when we look back at the respective careers of Elvis and Buddy Holly, the playing fields were certainly far from level.

Was it ever really Elvis versus Buddy?

It was the late Beatle George Harrison who said that, during the emergence of rock & roll in Britain, you were either a Buddy Holly or an Elvis Presley fan, and indeed there really was a period during late 1958 when that briefly held true. The Crickets had just become the first group to have three consecutive singles reach the Top 5 of the UK charts and their British tour in the March of that year had left an indelible mark on their fans, as well as on a generation of aspiring performers including Eric Clapton, Hank Marvin, Mick Jagger and Paul, John and George from the soon-to-be-formed Beatles. In the United States however, the situation was very different and any rivalry with Elvis didn't come from Holly, but rather the homely and squeaky-clean Pat Boone.

Boone it was who had dominated the US pop charts from 1955, and it seemed during the dynamic explosion that heralded Elvis' arrival on the national scene that he was the very antithesis of the too-good-to-be-true

---

[*] Coincidentally, Elvis — a big fan of Johnnie Ray — went on to score a US Top 20 hit with the song in 1964, having originally recorded it in 1960 for the *Elvis is Back!* album shortly after coming out of the army. That said, he was also a big Clyde McPhatter/Drifters fan, and they were the first to have a hit with this Lincoln Chase composition way back in 1954, so possibly that was the major influence.

crooner with his white bucks and gleaming smile.

Conversely, in his own country Buddy Holly was just one of dozens of other chart acts who were around during the late Fifties, and there was seemingly little to set him apart from the pack — certainly not as a potential heart-throb. But the purpose of this book is most definitely *not* to compare Elvis Presley with Buddy Holly, or draw any conclusions as to their abilities or even their respective contributions to the history of popular music.

If statistics alone were the sole criterion, then a quick 'no contest' would immediately be rung up, as Presley sold around 150 million records up to his death (one billion worldwide to date is sometimes quoted), racking up 146 *Billboard* 'Hot 100' hits in the US alone. He also made over thirty motion pictures, was awarded untold gold and platinum records and, as if that wasn't enough for any performer, also received three Grammy Awards along the way. Notwithstanding all these prestigious musical honours, it seems he was particularly flattered to be voted one of the 'Top Ten Young Men Of America' for 1971 — an award that he collected in person (a rare occurrence for Elvis). A further statistic to conjure with is that it was estimated a few years ago that there were still around five hundred Elvis Presley fan clubs in operation throughout the world, and many more if one includes today's proliferating websites.

If we contrast this with Buddy Holly's fame in purely statistical terms, his achievements were particularly slender — even if deceptively so. Indeed, it comes a something of a shock to note just how few hits he had, particularly in his own country: a mere eleven in comparative *Billboard* terms, including two posthumous entries and none after the end of the Fifties.

But to redress the balance somewhat, Holly did have some classic songwriting credits to his name and would also become an influential figure to many of the British groups that followed in the Sixties including the Beatles, the Searchers, the Rolling Stones and many others. The Texan even featured prominently in the UK 'Top Instrumentalist' polls of the day — a tribute to his mastery of the Fender Stratocaster, which he undoubtedly helped to pioneer in rock & roll circles as luminaries such as the aforementioned Hank Marvin and Eric Clapton have readily attested. It is said that, shortly before his death, he had been approached by Fender to have a solid-bodied guitar carry his name. These days, that's quite a common practice, and Fender have produced customised guitars that bear the names of Hendrix, Clapton, Stevie Ray Vaughan, Buddy Guy and several others, but in the pioneering Fifties it was virtually unheard of.

To hark back to the third paragraph of this section, no real comparisons between Holly and Presley are sought here; rather, the intention is to retell and celebrate their lives while pausing awhile to ponder on those early meetings and wonder whether it was luck, destiny or some other factor that threw them together so momentarily back then. If there is to be any karmic dimension to our musings, then perhaps 'destiny' is the choice that we will be drawn towards, especially if we ponder the thought that perhaps nothing in this world ever really happens just through random chance.

What we do know is that Elvis burst on the scene dramatically in 1956 — so much so that pundits have likened his impact on Fifties music as equal to the combined impact of the Beatles, the Rolling Stones and Bob

Dylan on the musical landscape of the Sixties. The comparison with the impression that Buddy Holly and the Crickets made at the same time is pretty stark, although they did briefly become chart-toppers on both sides of the Atlantic. But in reality they were 'just another' American chart act and, although some record buyers of the time no doubt thought the group were special (as you may guess this writer did), it wasn't until years later that we realised that the slow-burning fuse which Holly's voice had lit was still smouldering in the hearts of many a listener.

'The greatest voice in rock & roll' according to one perceptive female rock critic of the late Sixties, but she was one of very few to identify and highlight in print Holly's impact and unique talent up to that point. To many others, it bordered on the distasteful to listen to and champion the work of dead singers — an attitude that persisted for a while but is seldom taken as a serious viewpoint these days (as witness the posthumous careers of Roy Orbison, John Lennon, Freddie Mercury and many others).

It was eventually to become apparent to a much wider audience that, although Buddy Holly had departed this world in the physical sense, his voice and the music he created were still with us. Surprisingly — and this is still difficult to analyse or pinpoint exactly why — neither his unique voice nor his sound have dated as much as those of many of his contemporaries.

Moreover, it's an unarguable fact that you can take almost any comparable Fifties artist whose chart history completely eclipses that of Buddy Holly to prove that chart success alone is neither a guarantee of career longevity, nor a benchmark for greatness. For example, the handful of 'Hot 100' hits that Holly amassed in the US doesn't even come close to the twenty-five that Frankie Avalon (remember him?) had, or the thirty that the now little-remembered Bobby Rydell notched up between 1959 and 1965. But perhaps that just reinforces the view that statistics alone are not and never will be the sole arbiter of an artist's stature, but rather that it's something much more indefinable and of which chart success is a mere fragment.

Sadly, whatever it is, we're not going to find the answer laid out within these pages, although by the end of this book some readers may have some thoughts of their own on the subject. Perhaps Buddy's parents came closest in the few lines they penned for the sleeve of his posthumous *Reminiscing* album and which are quoted in the summing up during the final chapter.

At least the legacy of both our subjects is now assured in many varied ways. With Holly, the fact that the stage musical of his life, *Buddy*, is still running in many countries a dozen years after it first hit the stage in the late Eighties is testimony enough, whilst additionally his former group, the Crickets, is still touring regularly some forty years on and drawing audiences all over the world. As the badge stickers are apt to say rather straightforwardly 'BUDDY HOLLY LIVES', and any time a fan listens to one of those timeless classics or watches the stage musical this still rings true.

Curiously, one of the things both singers have in common is the fact that their fans frequently use the tag BUDDY HOLLY/ELVIS LIVES. Contrast this with contemporaries such as Bill Haley: Haley was one of the indisputable greats of rock & roll, yet one seldom encounters a 'BILL HALEY LIVES' sticker! (If we wish to introduce a spooky element, we could also reflect on the quirky fact that 'ELVIS' is actually an anagram of 'LIVES'.)

With Presley, the pointers to his continuing popularity are likewise many and varied, albeit quite different. It goes without saying that his fan base was and remains so much larger than Holly's, whilst the fact that only a quarter of a century has elapsed since his passing means that we've had less time for his impact and memory to fade. Nothing can change the reality that the Seventies will forever remain nearer to the surface of our memories than the Fifties. Why, even as recently as 2001 you could have gone to London to watch the King perform on a giant video screen whilst most of his backing artists from the Seventies accompanied him in what was advertised as a 'live' concert! In some ways, it seems almost as if he's never gone away at all. (This is never more apparent than in Las Vegas, where it seems every other casino boasts an Elvis impersonator!)

Several musicals based on his life have also been performed in the West End over the years and one feels that we haven't seen the last of these. Meanwhile, his Graceland home in Memphis has remained one of the top tourist attractions in the US ever since it was opened to the public in 1982, attracting around 700,000 visitors annually — even if it's more a testament to the garish interior design fashions of the Sixties and Seventies than to the man himself. His records likewise continue to sell, even if the regular single hits are no longer there, and his back catalogue is repackaged endlessly and quite imaginatively. Of course, out-takes, rehearsals and alternative masters from recording sessions continue to surface, as does live material from the concert years. Even as this book goes to press, Elvis is again at the top of the UK charts with *A Little Less Conversation (JXL remix)*.

So, it seems that 'ELVIS LIVES' too, and the only marked difference to Holly is that a few sad individuals might actually believe it a bit too literally. Presumably they won't be reading this book, being too busy researching reported sightings or else hoping that one day their hero might be cloned from the ancient wart that was supposedly removed from his finger and retained for posterity! Visit some of the many wacky websites that are around and you'll read that Elvis and Bigfoot are probably one and the same individual. Or why not join the First Presleytarian Church of Elvis the Divine? Mercifully, the true Elvis has no connection with the nonsense that flourishes in this internet age.

Back in the real world, it's surely enough for the overwhelming majority of us to applaud the respective contributions both men made to the music during their lifetimes as being a full and sufficient memorial to their names (as well as the statues that have now been erected in their honour in Memphis and Lubbock).

So at last to our story. Just what was it like in the USA as the remaining days of 1954 ebbed away, and what were our two protagonists up to at that point? Although it often seems to the general public that an artist in almost any walk of life suddenly makes their debut centre-stage fully formed, that's seldom the case and a long road has usually been travelled, often stretching back over many years. 'Paying your dues' it's sometimes called, and that certainly held true for both Elvis Presley and Buddy Holly as we'll discover.

Musical Interlude #1

> *An Empty Cup* and *You've Got Love,*
> both recorded by the Crickets (with Buddy
> Holly on lead vocals) in the Officers' Club
> Lounge at Tinker Air Force Base, Oklahoma
> City.
> *Tryin' To Get To You* recorded by Elvis
> Presley at Sun Studios, Memphis in July 1955.

There's a small but intense link between the titles mentioned above, the common denominator being that other 'late great' from the rock & roll era, Roy Orbison (1936–88).

The Holly titles were two of four numbers cut on portable equipment at a USAF base during a brief gap in the *Biggest Show Of Stars For 1957* tour and were the only Roy Orbison compositions he ever recorded.

Orbison, who came from Vernon, Texas (just south of Lubbock) had been a committed rock & roller ever since seeing Elvis perform at the *Big D Jamboree* in Dallas in 1955, but even at this early stage of his career was already displaying a flair for ballads. Through a quirk of fate, he started life as a recording artist at Norman Petty's studio a year or so before Buddy Holly. (Although Roy and Buddy never ran into each other at Clovis, their paths did cross on one occasion which he recalled in the MPL television documentary, *The Music Lives On*: 'I only really got to know Buddy Holly that day. It was from early morning to early morning. We were kindred souls, we became quite close.')

When the Crickets started getting hits, Roy was naturally more than happy for the boys to cut some of the compositions he had left at Clovis with Norman Petty.

An Empty Cup was one of his earliest efforts, recorded with his group, the Teen Kings (formerly the Wink Westerners) in late 1956 or early

1957. *You've Got Love* (co-written by Orbison, Petty and the Teen Kings' guitarist, Johnny 'Peanuts' Wilson) was cut by Wilson in the summer of 1957 for the flip of his Petty-produced rockabilly classic, *Cast Iron Arm*.

As for Presley's *Tryin' To Get To You*, this was a fairly obscure 1954 recording by a black vocal group called the Eagles which Elvis heard and liked. He performed it regularly at live dates throughout Texas in the mid-Fifties — which is almost certainly how Orbison first got to hear the song.

Both men subsequently recorded the number during 1955, with Orbison getting his out first on the small Je-Wel label as the flip side of *Ooby Dooby* — possibly the first rock & roll record Norman Petty ever produced. Presley's version was cut around the same time in the Sun studios but remained on the shelf while Sam Phillips negotiated the sale of his contract to RCA, eventually surfacing in March 1956 as a track on his first album, *Elvis Presley*. The song remained a perennial favourite of the singer, who continued performing it in concert right up to the very end.

Although Elvis was both a fan and friend of the 'Big O' — he later presented him with one of his lavish belts — it's surprising to note that he rarely sang any of his material on stage, even though the latter's dramatic ballads would surely have suited his style. Surprisingly, he didn't even try out *Blue Angel* — a huge hit for Orbison in 1960 — despite the fact that he found the spiritual colour blue irresistible and recorded a quite disproportionate number of tracks with 'blue' in the title. Who knows why? Perhaps Orbison's songs were just too closely associated with their composer, though it is also a fact that Presley kept to a familiar tried-and-tested playlist in those later Vegas years.

To round off this link, it's worth also mentioning that Orbison went on to recut *Ooby Dooby* at the Sun Studios in 1956. The remake gave him his first US chart hit, though he would have to wait nearly four more years before he made his big breakthrough with a brand new sound. Those 'dum-dum-dum-dumbee-do-wahs' might look pretty silly when written out on the printed page, but they helped to sell a million when used as back-up vocals on *Only The Lonely*!

- CHAPTER 2 -

Learning The Game

Rhythmic stirrings from the Deep South

In the early Fifties, the teenage Buddy Holly and Elvis Presley were living in the southern United States, albeit separated on the map by the state of Arkansas, which translates to over seven hundred miles at that particular conjuncture. They may they have been separated in a physical sense, but they were certainly about to be thrust together musically. However, before we turn to those important early meetings in Lubbock in 1955, let's firstly see what each man had or hadn't achieved at the precise moment when the calendar pages for 31 December 1954 were about to yellow and become yesterday's news.

Certainly, there's no doubt at all that Presley was the man of the moment while Holly was the acolyte trying to grab onto his shimmering coat-tails in the hope that whatever young Elvis had done would rub off on him too. This he would have a real chance to discover during the coming year, when his hero seemed to be always passing through Lubbock, Texas on one or other of those early tours. By this time, Holly himself was already gigging around locally, although he was technically still a student at Lubbock High.* Whenever Elvis hit town, Buddy was right there too: watching, learning, taking it all in, akin to a craftsman learning his trade. But we're jumping forward a year — let's back up a little.

It was actually as long ago as the summer of 1953 that the Tupelo, Mississippi Flash walked into Sam Phillips' Sun studio in Memphis to cut a two-sided demo** of *My Happiness* and *That's When Your Heartaches Begin*, both ballads. Asked by Sam's assistant, Marion Keisker, what sort of music he played, he famously responded: 'I don't sound like nobody.'

Within a year, he proved this by laying down several groundbreaking sides that inextricably fused the sound of hillbilly with the rhythms of R&B into a completely new kind of music. His first two Sun singles, *That's All Right (Mama)* and *Good Rockin' Tonight***, came out in July and September 1954

---

* The Thomas S. Lubbock High School to which Buddy went in the early Fifties was one of two high schools in the city of Lubbock and drew its students from the white population; Dunbar High catered for black students.

** Although Elvis indicated to Marion Keisker that the record was to be a present for his mother (though not a birthday present, as has often been misreported), it's likely that his main motivation in making it was simply to hear what he sounded like.

*** The original had been reasonably successful for its composer Roy Brown in 1947, but it was a bigger hit still the following year when covered by Wynonie Harris. Sadly, due to poor distribution, many successful recordings by black artists in these early *(continued overleaf)* and started getting a little reaction around the Memphis area, even if those in the outside world were to remain blissfully unaware of his existence for a while yet.

Holly meanwhile had no recording contract, although he'd already cut a handful of songs at home and at the local radio station, KDAV. Sometime in late 1954 or early 1955, he also cut some hillbilly-styled demos at the small, unknown Nesman Studio upstate in Wichita Falls, close to the Oklahoma border.

By the time 1955 arrived, Elvis had already got to both first and second bases with tours and recordings behind his belt, while Buddy was still stuck at that initial 'yearning and hoping' stage. But if yearning could be deemed any kind of yardstick, he *had* made a start of sorts, and there's no doubt at all that he got to hear those early Elvis Sun singles sometime during 1954 and realised that a hick country repertoire — with the occasional inclusion of a gospel number for the older contingent amongst his God-fearing audiences — would no longer cut the mustard. Overnight things began to get a whole lot more rhythmic!

Decision time

It seems certain that, back in 1954, both Elvis in Memphis and Buddy in Lubbock had twin obsessions on their minds that momentarily threatened to derail their dreams of a musical career and an escape from their humdrum Southern existences. Should it need spelling out in stark terms, the choice was between two very real adolescent pleasures: girls or music.

For Elvis, this was not just any sort of music of course, but the new, exciting, vibrant sound that he would help to create, and for which he would become — for a while at least — the major conduit.

But the dilemma was nevertheless very real: Elvis, his hormones racing, was having regular dates with an exceedingly attractive young lady named Dixie Locke, whom he'd first met at the local roller rink and who had became his high school sweetheart. Why, she'd even been his prom date that year, which was a mighty big deal back then in Fifties' America. So, had he already made the choice and chosen girls — or one in particular, in the attractive shape of Dixie, that most Southern of all names and one that must surely have appealed greatly to him? Maybe his music was taking off and maybe other girls were hanging around trying to bring complications, but Elvis and Dixie seemed drawn to each other.

For a while they were inseparable and the possibility of a life together surely beckoned them. Whether or not this would have blunted his musical desires is not known, and ultimately it seems not to have been an issue that led to any deep discussion between the two of them. Rather, it would appear that Elvis was almost subconsciously drawn towards music, and in pursuing it

---

days were only regional hits, their sales usually being insufficient to take them into the national charts. The label of 'race music' was thankfully to disappear in the Fifties thanks to enlightened individuals such as Jerry Wexler of Atlantic Records who coined the phrase 'rhythm & blues' while working on *Billboard* as a journalist, thereby helping to remove some of the stigma which existed.

in an all-consuming way inevitably broke the link with Dixie. It wasn't a clean break, however, and Dixie continued to visit with his parents until the autumn of 1955, although in reality their lives had effectively begun to go in different directions a good twelve months earlier. But, if it was an intensely sad time for one eighteen year old Memphis girl, she would unwittingly earn the gratitude of millions of future fans.

After Dixie, Elvis had another early and equally intense relationship with June Juanico, whom he met when on tour in her home town of Biloxi, Mississippi. She later wrote a thoughtful and highly-readable memoir of those times in a book entitled *Elvis In The Twilight Of Memory*, but this relationship also ended when he was unable to balance affairs of the heart with the demands of his career.

Down in Texas meanwhile, the situation wasn't really so very different for another young man where affairs of the heart were concerned. Buddy had briefly met a young Echo McGuire back in elementary school, but lost touch when his family moved out of the area. It must have seemed like kismet to eventually renew their acquaintance in Lubbock High upon his return following another house move and find that the original attraction was still there for both of them. Unlike Elvis, the obstacle was not really the music (although Echo apparently wasn't particularly keen on Buddy's), but rather her religious persuasion — an important factor in Southern society back then, and particularly for Echo.

She was a devout member of the Church Of God[*], whilst Buddy and his family all attended the local Tabernacle Baptist Church in Lubbock — both, it seems, much different in their Christian outlook. Enlightened readers today might think in terms of 'one God, many paths', but this was the fundamentalist Deep South in the Fifties and enlightenment and self-attainment weren't exactly floating around in the warm Texas ether. For Buddy and Echo the path was never going to be other than difficult, and so it proved just a few years later when they went their separate ways shortly before Buddy went off to Nashville to record — of which we'll learn more later. The link which had begun to weaken finally broke in late 1955, when Echo went away to the Christian College at Abilene to pursue her studies.

It is also likely that both Elvis and Buddy saw other girls despite having steady dates. Isn't it often the case that young men develop split minds on the subject and convince themselves that they are not really being unfaithful by such actions? That's if they ever paused to think deeply about it at all that is! All the more surprising then, that the swirling musical thoughts in their heads somehow managed to overwhelm even their rampaging hormones: indisputable proof that their music — it had no precise name or label back in 1954 — had something irresistible about it that couldn't be denied and was destined to burst through.

Thanks to his early start, Elvis was much further forward in this respect than Buddy, and his coming together that July with Scotty Moore and Bill Black in the recording studio at 706 Union Avenue, Memphis (with good

---

[*] As a child, Elvis Presley attended another branch of the 'Holy Rollers', the First Assembly Of God Church — one of the earliest points that music entered his life.

Elvis, Bill and Scotty in the Sun studio with Sam Phillips.

ol' Sun Records boss Sam Cornelius Phillips as the facilitator) had been nothing short of a miracle of chance. 'Pure accident' if we are to believe Moore, but a defining moment nonetheless. The musical blue touchpaper had been lit and was beginning to fizz, even if those involved were not fully aware of what they were about to unleash.

Certainly Phillips realised that he was onto something big. After spending several years recording local black talent, he'd come to the firm conclusion that 'the negroes were the only ones who had any freshness left in their music. If I could find a white boy who had the negro sound and feel, I could make a million dollars.' Now his dream had suddenly become reality, and he threw all his energies into promoting his new discovery. It's telling that, following the appearance of *That's All Right (Mama)* b/w *Blue Moon Of Kentucky* on 19 July 1954, there were no other releases on Sun until 10 November apart from Elvis' second single, *Good Rockin' Tonight* (issued 22 September).

For the second half of that year, Scotty Moore also acted as Elvis' manager, as it had become increasingly obvious that someone was needed to sort out the bookings that were beginning to flood in. It was to be January 1955 before Bob Neal, a deejay on WMPS in Memphis, would take over and allow him to concentrate on his first love — that of being a musician and a member of the Elvis Presley Trio. Along with fellow Memphian Dewey Phillips on WHBQ, Neal was the prime champion of Presley's music in those formative early days.

With the scene now set, it's time to take a look at the other young men that surrounded Elvis and Buddy in 1954, as it's for certain that no-one ever really acts in isolation. Who else formed part of the musical brew that would draw on the roots of various types of music to help form this exciting new hybrid?

Part of that mixture was, of course, drawn from the popular mainstream music of the day, while other ingredients were added from more obscure country & western and rhythm & blues influences. For sure, there were many elements that would be blended within this new musical concoction and countless books have since been written on the subject.* We will try and avoid that cul-de-sac here while acknowledging that rock & roll came into being around that time. As to who coined the phrase 'rock & roll' or became its first protagonist, either deliberately or otherwise, is an argument for others and not this author. Who knows, perhaps it was via that delightfully Transatlantic word 'happenstance'?

Instead, let's concentrate our thoughts on those bit-part players who shared the stage with Elvis and Buddy Holly back then and who, if not exactly king-makers, were certainly important ingredients within that simmering musical flux.

Elvis and his sidemen

Although no-one realised it at the time — and certainly not Elvis — 1954 was to be one of the pivotal years of his life. Indeed, the effect he was having on personal appearances was already beginning to ripple out from Tennessee.

October 1954 was to be a particularly significant month for him, and with hindsight it's perhaps the moment when his career could have somehow shoehorned itself into the C&W field if his searingly original talent hadn't been too incandescent to control. It was also around this time that attempts to categorise music in the South became inextricably tangled up with the thorny issue of segregation, shortly to erupt into major civil rights confrontations. The black influences in Presley's music certainly caused some confusion. In Memphis, the press had to settle for saying that he was 'achieving popularity in the rural rhythm field' — which was probably as near as they could get to describing his sound without using the traditional term 'race'.

So, what were those major events of October 1954? Well, on 2 October, Elvis performed for the first and only time on the *Grand Ole Opry* radio show broadcast by WSM out of Nashville and — fortunately for the world of popular music — the country audience reportedly wasn't ready for him.

His reception was either lukewarm, cool, stunned or just plain hostile depending on which of the reports one happens to read — and many of those descriptions have since been revised, as it certainly makes for a better story

---

* Dawson & Propes' *What Was The First Rock & Roll Record?* (see *Bibliography*) identifies fifty records — dating from the immediate post-War period up until Elvis appeared on the scene — that could all lay claim to being the first authentic rock and roll recording!

to have the future King Of Rock & Roll getting barracked! What *is* certain, is that the Elvis Presley Trio (as they were then billed) didn't carry all before them during that first appearance. It even seemed that a repeat scenario might take place just two weeks later when they made another debut on KWKH's less staid *Louisiana Hayride* in Shreveport, but by the time the second show went out they'd won the audience over. El and the boys went on to sign up for a year as regular members of the *Hayride* — a contract that was subsequently renegotiated (with an elevenfold increase in pay to $200 per appearance) by Colonel Tom Parker* shortly after he officially took over as Presley's 'special adviser' in August 1955.

Unlike the young Buddy Holly, who always had a gaggle of musicians around him in Lubbock, Elvis Presley cut a decidedly solitary figure. Although he had often toted his guitar around Memphis and had occasionally played with friends, he had never really been in any kind of group** until things started to happen at Sun. The sidemen situation was reasonably clear cut from the outset, in that the trio was initially billed as 'Elvis Presley with Scotty and Bill' or 'Elvis Presley with the Blue Moon Boys' (a reference to *Blue Moon Of Kentucky* — the powerful flip of their first Sun release).

'Scotty and Bill' were of course the taciturn Winfield Scott Moore III on lead guitar and the ever-lively William Patton Black on slap bass. Although they had both already made Elvis' acquaintance several years earlier, they joined forces with the singer through the good offices of Sun boss Sam Phillips, giving up lesser work with a local country outfit called the Starlite Wranglers, who had had an unsuccessful release on Sun that May backing the little-known singer, Doug Poindexter.

Although a few of those later Presley Sun singles also featured drums, the drummer most associated with Elvis, D.J. Fontana, wasn't fully involved with the trio at this point. In fact, he didn't appear on any of Presley's Memphis recordings, but was initially based over in his home town of Shreveport — the venue from which the *Louisiana Hayride* was broadcast each week, and with whom he played as staff drummer. He eventually joined Presley's group in August 1955, and made a memorable recording debut in New York in January of the following year on the session which produced *Heartbreak Hotel*, Elvis' first national chart-topper.

But we have to remind ourselves that, during 1954, the focus was on the exciting (if drummer-less) trio of Elvis, Scotty and Bill, and it's hardly surprising that a spate of copyists emerged down South. Of these, the Johnny Burnette Rock'n'Roll Trio is the outfit whose name has lingered longest in the minds of rock & roll zealots, particularly in Britain. Indeed, it is sometimes argued over whether Johnny (who was a neighbour of Elvis' in Memphis) copied him or vice versa. Perhaps it was neither, simply two separate manifestations of a shared cultural experience. (A minor coincidence is that Johnny Black, Bill Black's brother, went on to play bass with the Johnny Burnette Trio, albeit not on their classic 1957 Coral recordings.)

---

* The reputation of the much-maligned honorary Colonel is such that in recent years when he died, a retrospective on his life was feelingly entitled a '*Sonofabituary*'!

** Earlier in the year, he had aspired to join an amateur Memphis gospel outfit called the Songfellows, but had been rejected.

Scotty, Elvis and Bill in action on the Louisiana Hayride, 1954.

Sadly, both Scotty and Bill — unhappy about being put on a set wage by Colonel Parker — left Elvis in September 1957 mid-way through his first wave of major success and never really got to share in much of the glory (or money) that might have come their way.

Buddy poses with his parents and Jack Neal (far right), circa 1953/54.

Buddy and his sidemen

As for Lubbockite Buddy Holly, who were his backing musicians at the corresponding point in his career? Well, the situation was decidedly more fluid than in Presley's case, and certainly more complex in view of the number of musicians involved. If many have subsequently claimed they played with Buddy in Lubbock — 'The Hub City Of The South Plains' as it's sometimes called — there were really only a handful of contemporaries that were in any sense permanent, and they are given a name-check here.

Although a recording contract was still two years away in 1954 and he wasn't even a professional musician at this point[*], music clearly already dominated Buddy's life. As he was shortly to be drawn to Elvis like the proverbial moth to a flame, so others would also begin to gravitate towards Buddy from around this period. With Presley, the attraction was a combination of the music with his image, dynamism and overall charisma; with Holly, it was quite simply down to his instrumental prowess and the plain fact that even at this stage he played guitar far better than just about anyone

---

[*] In Lubbock, an unofficial coterie had grown up around Cotton Club owner Tommy Hancock, who had formed a 'Club For Unappreciated Musicians' and even handed out membership cards. There was no fee, but it meant that the chosen local musicians would be welcomed into the club free of charge — quite a benefit. Of this illustrious small group, Sonny Curtis was member No.1, Buddy member No.4 and Jerry Allison No.5.

Sonny Curtis (fiddle), Bob Montgomery (acoustic guitar), Buddy Holly (electric guitar)
and Larry Welborn (bass) provide entertainment at the opening of
Rallo Henry's Superette, Lubbock on 1 June 1955.

else thereabouts, with the possible exception of Sonny Curtis, whose name crops up below. Meanwhile, those that knew Buddy at the time remember him getting a great sound from guitar, mandolin, banjo or ukelele. Why, if he'd been shown a plank of wood with a couple of strings attached, chances are he'd have got a tune out of that too!

It's perhaps an overstatement to call the shifting group of musicians Holly had around him in 1954 'sidemen' as such, there being much coming and going with up to ten individuals contributing in a variety of ways. Although this isn't intended as a reference book, it's probably easiest to tabulate some of the configurations that were around from about late 1953 to early 1955, bearing in mind that Buddy was still a full-time student at Lubbock High at this time. The list included:

- From 1953, the duo of Buddy & Jack (Holly and guitarist/pianist Jack Neal, who occasionally still plays today) appeared on radio and television shows, specialising in country and gospel material. Several years older than Buddy, Jack handled most of the lead vocals while Buddy sang harmony. In October 1953, they landed a regular thirty-minute spot on KDAV's *Sunday Party* (Lubbock's local interpretation of the *Grand Ole Opry* concept).

- The group name 'the 580 Ranch Hands' is mentioned by Buddy in a 1954 letter, but it seems this was the name used when Buddy & Jack appeared with backing musicians on KDAV ('580' being the station's wavelength).

- At high school, Buddy formed a group with Bob Montgomery (who went on to enjoy a long country music career as producer and publisher in Nashville) and bassist Larry Welborn. On one occasion, they won a school contest with *Flower Of My Heart*, a version of which was later made available on the *Holly In The Hills* album. This aggregation evolved into 'Buddy & Bob', who eventually took over from Buddy & Jack.

- In May 1954, the name 'the Rhythm Playboys' was used, and the group consisted of Buddy, Bob, Jack Neal and an obscure individual called David Bowen who probably got to lug the bass around!

- The earliest country demos that Buddy made circa 1954–55 featured Bob Montgomery on guitar, Larry Welborn or Don Guess on bass, and Sonny Curtis on fiddle.

- Guitarist Tinker Carlen is another personality from Lubbock who definitely hung around musically with Buddy around 1954, but his name doesn't figure in any group line-ups.

- Others that were about to enter the frame include the youthful, yet-to-be-famous Waylon Jennings* and the even younger Jerry Allison. (This being 1954, it was somewhat later before Joe B. Mauldin and Niki Sullivan — both familiar names to British fans — arrived on the scene.)

Buddy had met up with drummer Jerry Ivan Allison (known to his friends and fellow musicians as 'J.I.') as early as 1952, albeit they were mere school acquaintances and it would be some time before they teamed up to become musical buddies. As has already been mentioned, in those early days he would have been as likely to strap on a banjo as a guitar, and the music he performed was predominantly bluegrass or western swing — pretty standard fare in the part of Texas he was in. That's certainly the way Sonny Curtis remembers it being back in '52, when he and Buddy first met up and Sonny would join him on second guitar or — as often as not — the fiddle.

But back to Jerry, and for a frustrating time it literally depended on whether Elvis was using a drummer as to whether or not Jerry got to drum with Buddy. Certainly for a while, he continued playing with another local group — Cal Wayne & The Riverside Ranch Hands — of an evening while carrying on with his schooling during the day. But it wouldn't be too long before any indecision was swept away and his long-term association with Buddy got underway.

---

* Sonny Curtis and Waylon Jennings both deserve to be more than mere footnotes, as each went on to carve out a significant solo career, as detailed in the *Glossary*. Curtis, who was from Meadow, Texas balanced his career as a singer/guitarist in and out of the Crickets with an alternative existence as a highly successful songwriter responsible for such classics as *Rock Around With Ollie Vee, Walk Right Back, More Than I Can Say* and *I Fought The Law*. He remains the front-man with the Crickets as these words are written. Jennings, born in nearby Littlefield, was the Nashville rebel who crossed over into the pop charts in the Seventies, although he's probably best remembered as writer and performer of the theme music to the long-running *Dukes of Hazzard* TV show.

Buddy and Bob at grand opening of a local store, 1953.
Buddy is playing a banjo loaned to him by his brother Larry.

Having set the somewhat shifting scene above, it's now time to take a brief trip through the time tunnel and take a look at how both Elvis and Buddy arrived in 1954. Although their stories have been touched upon earlier, there's still a need to peel back a few more layers if we are to make sense of their lives and set the stage for their meetings.

Both had been born during the Thirties when the run-up to World War II was underway in Europe, even as Herr Hitler was beginning to flex his muscles as German Chancellor. Of course, for the two energetic toddlers all this had no meaning whatsoever, and even the adult inhabitants of Texas and Mississippi would most likely have been more interested in news from in and around their own locality, or within their county or state borders than on the global scene. They would certainly never have believed that a second World War would break out so soon after the first. But break out it did, and the potentially isolationist United States would again reluctantly find itself drawn into the deepening conflict on several fronts.

In the following two chapters, we'll cover those formative years for both Elvis and Buddy from the Thirties to the mid-Fifties, turning firstly to Elvis in his pre-Memphis days. Of course, he wasn't yet the King, the Hillbilly Cat, the Pelvis (the name he particularly hated), the King Of The Western Bop, the Memphis Flash, or really anything at all other than a youthful El whose twitching legs were still hardly fully formed.

Every source confirms the obvious — that he was tied firmly to his mother's apron strings at the outset — and that whole relationship is one that has been discussed in many writings over the years. In 1985, Elaine Dundy devoted a whole book to the subject, *Elvis And Gladys*, and although it's written from the outside looking in, it provides an illuminating insight into their relationship. In *Early Elvis: The Tupelo Years* Bill E. Burk insists that, although mother and son were close, Gladys did not — as is oft quoted — walk him to school! It can be seen from this that the life and times of Elvis Presley continue to get analysed in considerable detail.

Whatever the depth of their relationship was, we know that in those earliest days surprisingly few musical thoughts were running through the mind of the young Elvis. But it seems he always had the feeling that he had a destiny to fulfil, even if he was uncertain how it would come about or even what form it would take! Indeed, it seems odd that, over the years, many famous individuals whose early lives seemed particularly mundane have had a second sight whereby they knew that something, sometime was going to happen and catapult them into a parallel universe of fame and fortune. However, let's not digress but instead go back to the Tupelo shack where Elvis was raised and reprise those childhood years to see what pointers there were, if any, that he would develop into such an extraordinary musical presence.

Musical Interlude #2

I Forgot To Remember To Forget recorded by Elvis Presley on 11 July 1955 at Sun Studio, Memphis, originally released on Sun on 1 August 1955 and reissued by RCA in 1956.
The same title recorded by Buddy Holly on acetate at radio station KLLL in Lubbock probably during 1955.

Presley's recording (coupled with *Mystery Train*) was his fifth and final Sun single. Released in August 1955, it reached No. 7 in the *Cash Box* country chart but, like his previous efforts, failed to cross over into the national pop charts. The song was composed by Stan Kesler (who also co-wrote *I'm Left, You're Right, She's Gone*) and demoed* by future rockabilly legend Charlie Feathers, who shared the credits and the royalties.

It is known that Elvis performed it on stage while touring Texas during the first year of his career, and it quickly became a great favourite with the young Buddy Holly and doubtless many others. A country-styled outing, it was never a big hit for anyone, although it was subsequently recorded by the likes of Toni Arden, Johnny Cash and Jerry Lee Lewis.

When RCA took over Presley's contract in November 1955, they quickly reissued all five of his Sun singles. This one enjoyed the greatest success, briefly topping the US country charts in February 1956 thanks to the label's better distribution, and in spite its earlier healthy sales.

---

* There is some disparity between Kesler's and Feathers' accounts of what happened: Kesler (who was steel guitarist with Clyde Leoppard's Snearly Ranch Boys) says he enlisted Feathers' help because he wanted a good demo of the song to present to Sam Phillips. Feathers (whose recollections were always somewhat fanciful) always claimed that Kesler presented him with an incomplete song which he finished off and arranged.

In contrast, the Holly version has never been heard since the Fifties, when it was often played by local radio station KLLL as the singer's popularity around the Lubbock area grew. Although at one time the acetate was thought to have been destroyed, it is now known to still exist although it has been rendered unplayable by deliberate deep scratching (the mutilation was apparently carried out at Holly's request after he signed to Decca in 1956, to avoid possible disputes over copyright infringement). With the technology that exists today, one wonders if a listenable transcription could perhaps be made from it after all?

Oddly enough, almost the reverse of the above story obtains for the two singers with respect to another country title, *Gone*. Written by Smokey Rogers, the number was first recorded by Ferlin Husky (under the pseudonym 'Terry Preston') for Capitol in 1952 and became a country hit. Holly loved the song and recorded a demo of it in Lubbock in the closing weeks of 1956, which was later released on the 1964 *Showcase* album. For his part, Elvis is known to have performed the song on the *Louisiana Hayride* and may even have recorded it at Sun, though if he did, it has so far failed to surface.

It sometimes seems strange that recordings are said to have 'disappeared', but it should be remembered that back in those days recording tape was felt to be more valuable than it is today, and was therefore often reused. If that meant erasing or recording over what was originally on the reel, then that was just too bad! Early takes of the classic *Rave On* disappeared like this, and some of the material that Elvis laid down at Sun and RCA doubtless went the same way.

- CHAPTER 3 -

Gum Pond to Memphis

What's in a name?

It may be a deceptively simple name, but Elvis Presley has always seemed somehow exotic — not only to the outside world where the words 'foreign' and 'exotic' are perhaps synonymous, but even to Americans themselves where names like Dwight D. Eisenhower or Nelson Rockefeller scarcely raise an eyebrow.

Of course, 'Presley' itself as a surname is not rare — there are three in my English home town telephone directory alone. Similarly, the names 'Elvis' and 'Aaron' are not totally unknown in the South, even if they are uncommon.* So, how has the name itself become more than just the sum of its parts? What has endowed the name Elvis Aaron Presley with such a seemingly magical quality? If it's difficult to explain, it's equally hard to deny it as a fact. From the very outset of his career, his baptismal names when taken together seem to have exerted a power that would surely have been impossible had they been as mundane as James Ray Smith or Terry John Hood (to pluck other surnames from the Presley family tree and prefix them with more popular Christian names of the day).

Did Elvis make a conscious decision to use his real name as his stage name? Certainly, it was common at that time for performers in the States to adopt pseudonyms. Many (such as Anthony Dominick Benedetto alias Tony Bennett) did it to smooth over their ethnic backgrounds in an effort not to alienate any segment of the complex ethnic flux that has made up the continental United States of America these past few hundred years. Others simply did it because their real names were too cumbersome or difficult to pronounce. Of course, there were many others who used their own name for both their private and public personas, so Elvis certainly wasn't unique in that respect. However, in hindsight, it was certainly an unusual name for the bill stickers of the day to cope with and announcers to get their larynxes around. Indeed, he quickly became known as 'the kid with the funny name' and would invariably be asked to repeat it. On one of his earliest shows — with Slim Whitman in Memphis — he was listed as 'Ellis Presley' on posters advertising

---

* Not unexpectedly, Elvis (meaning 'all wise' in the translation from the original Scandinavian) is very much the rarer of the two and was also the middle name of his father, Vernon. It seems that unusual names in the Presley family were commononplace by the time Elvis arrived, with a 'Vester' and a 'Delta' present among other branches. In contrast, Aaron is decidedly biblical, being the name of Moses' elder brother. Certainly, Elvis was intrigued by his unusual names and devoted time looking for a meaning to them as a part of his spiritual quest.

the event, while on other occasions he became 'Alvis'.

It's also worth mentioning at this point that it wasn't just us Brits that thought the name Elvis had an exotic ring about it. Band member Scotty Moore has said that, when he first heard the name, it sounded to him like something out of a science fiction comic! Interestingly, the late Lester Bangs, US critic of *Rolling Stone* magazine, once opined that the only credible explanation for Elvis was that he came from another planet! Meanwhile, singer Mac Davis (who hails from Lubbock and, coincidentally, composed *In The Ghetto*), could only account for the appearance of Buddy Holly in the midst of the Texas outback by suggesting that maybe he too had been dropped down from outer space. Readers who feel that, in entering the Third Millennium there may be special beings on Earth amongst us (were Elvis and Buddy unknowingly such beings, one wonders) may have some thoughts on the subject!

But moving on, and back on terra firma, we'll shortly find ourselves transported back to Lubbock, Texas during 1955 when the lifelines of these two young musical comets intersected one with another and we'll get to envy that fly on those sweaty Cotton Club or Fair Park Coliseum walls. Before that, however, we're reprising the early life stories of Buddy and Elvis and taking a peek at their differing backgrounds.

Frankly, neither had that much in common with the other in the beginning, other than being contemporaries with a rare and developing talent which combined their love of music with a drive to succeed come what may.

In Memphis, Elvis had managed to work his way up from his position as a lowly apprentice at the M.B. Parker Machinists' Shop to a $42-per-week truck driver with Crown Electric (where his father had worked before him), when his career began to take off regionally during the course of 1954.

Over in Texas meanwhile, Buddy had managed to avoid serious employment beyond the brief 'work experience' attachments that cropped up towards the end of his high school days. However, he did help out in the family ceramic tile business from time to time, although this produced a serious impediment to developing his music, as anyone who has ever cut tile would know without much need of explanation. The occupational hazard being hinted at is known as 'strawberry fingers', which could easily have curtailed guitar-picking practice had Buddy let it. With or without the help of a plectrum, the strings still had to be pressed down firmly and it would have been an arduous process for sure. A worthier example of 'no pain, no gain' is hard to imagine!

But we touch here on the next chapter, the one about Buddy. This one's about Elvis and the first eighteen years of life that took him from what is often termed a shack in the former Gum Pond (the original name of Mississippi's East Tupelo, later renamed Presley Heights) across state lines to Graceland, the mansion in Memphis, Tennessee where he was to remain for the last twenty-four years of his life. The later years would bring much

---

* Both the Tupelo shack and of course Graceland are open to visitors these days, and although to call the latter a mansion might be an overstatement, the contrast between the two properties is total. When purchased in 1958, Graceland had cost a palatial $100,000 — a huge amount of money at that time.

Elvis' birthplace: The shack on Old Saltillo Road (now Elvis Presley Drive), Tupelo.

success, but mixed in with a fair dose of heartache which the singer tried to blot out by surrounding himself with the trappings of materialism while at the same time exploring the inner, more spiritual side of his nature, either in isolation or at the instigation of one of his entourage, hairdresser Larry Geller.

Of course, there's been a plethora of all things Presley-related published over the years, so to give a detailed life story and rehash all that's gone before would be both repetitive and unnecessary. Better perhaps to settle for a quick trawl through the landmarks and maybe emphasise some of the lesser-known facts that are oft-times tucked away or overlooked.

Such as what, for example? Well, for starters there really *was* an area of Tupelo on the edge of the black community known as Shake Rag with the intriguing name of Gum Pond, and it's around there that the young Elvis was brought up. Anyone who craves real depth has probably already found this out by wading through the definitive two-part biography by the American author Peter Guralnick published in recent years. It's written with great compassion, but at an overall one thousand pages it's daunting to all except the discerning or diehard fan. Another who has written with great depth and insight into all things Elvis is the American Greil Marcus, whose works are also highly recommended. Both authors are far removed from the wealth of hangers-on who have written those '*I Was Elvis' Nurse/Dietician/Go-fer/etc*' memoirs that still crop up at depressingly regular intervals.

Having put down enough markers for now, the aim of this section of potted bio is not to sensationalise — the life of Elvis reads like a fairytale anyway — but rather provide a concise and factual overview of the main events in the singer's life from his birth in 1935 to around the time in 1955 when he and Buddy Holly first met. As previously stated, we'll try and also give due attention to any other neglected snippets that may have been overlooked in the past.

Elvis with his parents on the set of 'Loving You', 1957.

Vernon and Gladys

It's time we took a brief look at Vernon and Gladys Presley to see if in so doing any clues are thrown up as to why two such apparently ordinary folk should produce such a phenomenal offspring. That wording is used quite deliberately. Elvis may have his detractors, but few would deny that he became a potent musical symbol whose following has shown little sign of diminishing, even if his days as a chart presence, like his recording career, are effectively a thing of the past. Nonetheless, the author suspects that an Elvis renaissance will take place at some point, although — come to think of it — he's never really gone away, has he?

So, what was it in the genes of the plump, sleepy-eyed Gladys and the wiry Vernon that coalesced to produce Elvis? It would take a brave man to fully answer that, and certainly someone other than a geneticist. Maybe there were some musical spores floating over that part of the US that could provide the clue?

Why? Well, at the same time that Elvis was set to appear from the womb of Gladys Presley that January in 1935, Jerry Lee Lewis was being conceived down in Ferriday, Louisiana while Johnny Cash, Carl Perkins, Bob

Luman, Ronnie Hawkins, Sleepy LaBeef and a host of others had made, or were about to make their first appearance — all within a relatively small sector of the southern United States. Amazing coincidence it may have been, but surely one to ponder.

Gladys Love Smith (that's a pretty common surname, even in the USA) and Vernon Elvis Presley were married on 17 June 1933, the twenty-one year old bride — somewhat unusually — being four years the groom's senior. Although the United States strives to remain classless, it seems that the Presleys were somewhat poorer than the Smiths, though both were hard-working families based in and around the Mississippi border whose roots went back several generations to the Civil War and beyond.*

Although the exact mix of ancestry is not known, it appears that the Smith line had at least a trace of Jewish blood via Elvis' great-grandmother, Martha Tackett. So intrigued was he by this fact, that he later arranged for the 'Star of David' symbol to be added to his mother's tombstone — something, of course, that he took great care not to discuss with his father, who would have had no sympathy with such a notion.

The question of his lineage was a subject that particularly absorbed Elvis over the years as he continued his spiritual delving with the help of his hairdresser-guru, Larry Geller — who was himself Jewish and therefore able to assist and guide him in his search.

There was also a known American Indian ancestry** and it is a well-researched fact that Gladys had a many-times great-grandmother called Morning Dove White Mansell (1800–35), a full-blooded Cherokee whose tribe was indigenous to the Tennessee region.

But not all the ancestral lines for Vernon and Gladys are that clear-cut, and Vernon's father Jessie was apparently illegitimate, so to plot either family tree definitively is virtually impossible.

What is more certain, is that Vernon had a variety of manual jobs from the outset, with milkman, farm hand, painter, carpenter and truck-driver all listed by biographers. In a rare interview, Elvis himself stated: 'My daddy was a common laborer. He didn't have any trade, just like I didn't have.' (This of course was in the days before he hit the big time, when the need for Vernon to earn a living disappeared almost overnight. Thereafter, whatever work he did was on behalf of his son. He went on to manage Elvis' day-to-day finances at Graceland for years, which is perhaps surprising given his

---

* Although there are no obvious links back to foreign shores, the Presley family's provenance has been the subject of considerable genealogical debate over the years. In *Elvis: The Early Years — 2001, A Fact Odyssey* author Jim Curtin traces links back as far as the Sixteenth Century. Elsewhere, it has been asserted that Elvis had some Scottish ancestry in the Paisley area dating back to circa 1745, while in August 2000 *Record Buyer* magazine published details of a Welsh academic's claim that Elvis's forbears originated from the Mynydd Preseli region of Pembrokeshire in Wales! To cloud the picture even further, one Laurence Pressley, a bus driver from Darlington in the North-East of England, was last year presented with a certificate on ITV's *Find Your Family* confirming that he is the King's seventh cousin!

** It's an intriguing coincidence to the author that so many dynamic American singers have native American Indian blood in their veins. Chuck Berry, Bo Diddley, Marty Robbins, Johnny Cash, Johnny Horton, Marvin Rainwater, Buddy and Elvis are just a few random examples, and there are many others too in the jazz field. What is the magic ingredient — is it simply musical, or part of a greater spiritual dimension?

blue-collar background.)

Although living in poverty in a two-room 'shotgun shack' on Old Saltillo Road in East Tupelo, the couple somehow managed to struggle by and produce enough food for the table to sustain themselves. But when Gladys discovered in the spring of 1934 that she was pregnant, it must have been a worrying thought as to how they were going to feed all the expected mouths — though it is said they were not aware that twins were on the way.

If the parents-to-be felt any trepidation, it can only have been added to when the confinement started on that dark morning of 8 January 1935 and went on to last for several hours. The countdown to the event that was Elvis' birth was underway, and what a day of contrasting sadness and joy it would turn out to be for Gladys and Vernon (and, of course, a rather significant one too for the history of popular music).

Two becomes one

At the start, a possible tragedy seemed in the offing when the first* of the twin siblings, Jesse Garon, arrived stillborn and there was no alternative than to commit his remains to an unmarked plot at the nearby Priceville Cemetery, placed within a simple shoebox. The story is that the surviving brother, Elvis Aaron, would later make several attempts to find the exact location of the small grave without success. If, as it's always said, Jesse arrived in the world thirty-five minutes before his brother, that must have been a period of considerable anguish for Gladys and probably accounts for why she doted on Elvis from the day he weighed in at just five pounds until the day she died, having thankfully lived long enough to witness some of his earliest successes.

As for the stillborn twin, there is in the Meditation Garden at Graceland a mis-spelled marker for Jesse Garon, with the named incorrectly inscribed as 'Jessie'. Although the relationship between Elvis and his twin brother may not have been quite as dramatic as some reports would have us believe**, there's little doubt that he carried the name within his heart and maybe this loss was also partly responsible for the special empathy he had with his mother.

Another trauma for the Presley family was to occur around 1938 — Elvis was just three years old at the time — when Vernon wound up serving

---

* Interestingly, Vernon Presley's version of events differed from the doctor's records and he always insisted that Elvis was the first-born, and that the stillborn Jesse arrived shortly thereafter. According to Larry Geller, Elvis was convinced his dead twin was 'identical' and had several vivid dreams over the years that bore out this fact. In later years, Vernon — usually the most down-to-earth of individuals — also recalled that there was an unearthly and unaccountable blue light in evidence around the time Elvis was born!

** For example, in *The Illustrated Elvis Presley*, Geoffrey Giuliano writes: 'Gladys' obsession with her dead son made a deep impression on Elvis. Jesse was the constant, invisible presence, the wonder boy who would have grown up to be an achiever. His mother continuously urged Elvis to pray to Jesse and ask him for guidance. "He's our guardian angel in Heaven," she would tell him. "For as long as I can remember I've been talking to Jesse," Presley would later confess. His belief that half of his soul died at birth prevented him from enjoying his later success to the full. "If only Jesse were here," he lamented frequently throughout his life.'

time at the notorious Parchman Farm penitentiary in Mississippi for forgery. A charitable version of events would be that Mr. Presley, in association with two others, naïvely altered a company cheque in an attempt to boost his family's meagre income and got caught out for his pains. If he really was barely literate as has sometimes been claimed, then the incident merely serves to underline the extent of his desperation.

Aside from this isolated lapse of good character, it seems Gladys and Vernon were an ordinary if poor couple who had a good, solid marriage that lasted a full twenty-five years and until they were separated by death. Elvis, the extraordinary offspring of ordinary parents, would seldom if ever criticise his father and deferred to him affectionately as 'daddy' throughout his life. The consensus appears to be that they had a very close father/son relationship.

Vernon was to survive his son by almost two years, dying on 26 June 1979. In turn, Vernon's own mother (Minnie May Presley, known to Elvis by the nickname 'Dodger') didn't die until 1980, meaning that — most unusually — the three generations died in reverse order to the norm! Son, father and then grandmother.

Incidentally, as regards the Presleys' time in Tupelo, it's recorded that they lived at nine different addresses at least — and this doesn't take into account the fact that they were also occasionally been billeted with relatives. So, for the young Elvis life was forever on the move, even if initially the moves were all in and around the Tupelo, Mississippi area.

Clearly, the family's accommodation arrangements revolved around whatever jobs Vernon could get, and it was most certainly money — or rather lack of it — that eventually took the family in a beat-up 1939 Plymouth the hundred or so miles north across the border to Memphis, Tennessee in November 1948, when Elvis was just thirteen.

Whilst the city of Memphis wasn't the literal home of the blues, it had many connections with the music that gradually began to emerge at the end of the Nineteenth Century and these days boasts a statue of W.C. Handy (the self-styled 'Father Of The Blues') in Beale Street to push its credentials for the tourists that pass through. Again, several addresses are quoted for Elvis' homes in Fifties' Memphis, but the ones that have the most significance were surely the three years the family spent at Lauderdale Courts*, 185 Winchester Street (which takes us through to 1953) and 462 Alabama Avenue (where he was living in 1954 when Sam Phillips signed him to his Sun label).

The teenage Elvis attended Humes High School, an all-white establishment back in those days, and was already inseparable from the guitar he'd received a couple of years earlier for his eleventh birthday. It certainly accompanied him to most classes (whenever he could get away with it, that is).

Whilst Elvis could play that first guitar somewhat, it has to be acknowledged that his singing and playing did not make a particularly big impression on his classmates, despite the fact that he had won a prize in a

---

* Rockabilly singers Johnny and Dorsey Burnette also lived there, as did the family of his future bass-player, Bill Black, whom he met through his younger brother, Johnny.

Lauderdale Courts in the early 1950s.

talent contest at the *Mississippi-Alabama Fair & Dairy Show* for his rendition of Red Foley's tear-jerking *Old Shep* back in Tupelo when he was just ten years old. Most books claim it was a 2nd prize, but Guralnick quotes Elvis as saying he thinks he came fifth in the contest, while the author of *Early Elvis: The Tupelo Years*, Bill E. Burk, disputes whether he actually won anything at all. In the grand scheme of life it probably matters little which of such minor biographical facts are actually correct.

Whatever the truth of the matter, from the comments of his former schoolmates it would seem that Elvis only slowly grew in confidence and had to work hard to overcome his inherent shyness before his talent could shine through. Although he may not even have been aware of it himself, music was coming into his life from many different sources in those formative early years. Most times after the school week was over, he could be found at his local church or else hanging around the nearby black neighbourhood where

42

he absorbed the gospel sounds that were such a huge influence on his early life. So much so, that there's a telling quote from J.D. Sumner (leader of the Stamps gospel quartet who later performed with him), that all Elvis really wanted to do in life was to sing sacred music and, had he lived longer, he may have eventually turned in that direction — further evidence of his spirituality. It's certainly no coincidence that his Grammy awards were all for albums in the gospel or inspirational field, and there's often an intensity and quality in those performances that is absent from much of his other material. Listening nowadays to the Golden Gate Quartet's 1955 recording of *Swing Low, Sweet Chariot*, it's striking how similar the backing is

Elvis aged eighteen
(High School Graduation photo, June 1953).

to that employed on Presley's version — such is the strong and obvious influence.

Living in Memphis, he would also have been exposed to a wide variety of secular music on the local airwaves. Whilst mainstream white pop predominated, WMPS provided country programming, with Smilin' Eddie Hill's *Noontime Roundup* show (which thousands of workers regularly tuned into during their lunch break) being particularly influential. And, off course, WSM's *Grand Ole Opry* broadcasts from Nashville would also have been required listening.

The powerful WDIA ('America's only 50,000 watt Negro radio station') was also based in the city, and could well be how he first got to hear records such as Arthur 'Big Boy' Crudup's 1947 classic, *That's All Right* — a song that would remain with the youngster until the day he eventually stepped into the Sun studio to lay down his own version. Alternatively, he may have tuned into the city's other black music station, WLOK, or to Howlin' Wolf's broadcasts on KWEM from West Memphis across the river in Arkansas.

From 1948 onwards, there was also the anarchic Dewey Phillips on WHBQ, a white man who played the best R&B sounds around on his now-legendary *Red Hot & Blue* show, while future Sun supremo Sam Phillips — no relation, but very much a kindred spirit — presented a similarly eclectic mixture of jazz, blues and pop on his *Saturday Afternoon Tea Dance* on WREC.

Rock & roll was in the making, and there can be little doubt that all these influences gradually blended within Elvis' mind, inspiring him to create a potent new sound with which he would soon blow the world apart.

If the above few paragraphs seem inadequate to fully describe those first years of his life, that is because they really weren't that eventful even in hindsight, and at the time there still seemed little to mark him out from his contemporaries. So, just how on earth did this shy young man who first visited the Memphis Recording Service studio of Sam Phillips in 1953 to wax a couple of maudlin ballads come to undergo such an amazing metamorphosis that twelve months later he'd be known as 'the Hillbilly Cat' and electrify all who saw and heard him?

If a layman could describe how a butterfly emerges from the husk of a chrysalis, then perhaps one could come up with an answer. For this scribe, the explanation has to verge on the mystical, as there surely can't be a simple answer to this and the many other imponderables about Elvis, no matter how many words are written and however much his life is scrutinised under a microscope.

Musical Interlude #3

> ***Ready Teddy*, recorded by Elvis Presley in September 1956 at Radio Recorders Studio in Los Angeles.**
>
> **The same title recorded by Buddy Holly around May–July 1957 at the Norman Petty Recording Studio in Clovis, New Mexico.**

Neither of these recordings was intended as a single and both were versions of the original hit by Little Richard which had been written in 1956 by Bumps Blackwell (Richard's producer on the Specialty label) and John Marascalco. Holly's voice sounds hoarse on his recording of this frantic number as he strives to emulate Richard, while the released Presley version was Take 27 and had come at the end of a long three days of recording.

The unfortunate sequel is simply that, in the Seventies, a bootleg album of Presley's live recordings appeared containing what purported to be duets of Elvis and Buddy singing *Ready Teddy* and Elvis and Bill Haley cutting loose on another Little Richard classic, *Rip It Up*. However these 'duets' were not quite what they seemed and had been produced by simply playing one recording over the top of the other, with some fading in and out thanks to the wonders of stereo! The resulting cacophony has to be heard to be believed and isn't helped by the fact that each artist recorded their version at a different tempo. While the Holly/Presley duet may indeed be unique, it mostly reminds us that it's a music *business* we're talking about and offers proof that a market exists for almost anything where a known artist is involved.

On a similar if more tasteful note, an excellent duet was manufactured during the 1980s using the voices of Jim Reeves and Patsy Cline almost twenty years after their deaths. Their composite *Have You Ever*

Been Lonely was released and became a country hit, demonstrating what can be achieved if technology is coupled with a little love and care. More recently still, a duet was created between the late Nat 'King' Cole and his daughter Natalie, using Nat's original recording of *Unforgettable* from the Fifties and getting Natalie to overdub her part. This too met with great critical acclaim and became a deserved hit. Whilst money was still made along the way, one feels the motive was nowhere near as blatant as with the bootleg items mentioned above, and at least the listener got some enjoyment from the experience. Or perhaps the author is just being naïve.

All of this leads one to wonder whether at some time in the future we may yet hear 'new' recordings by long-dead artists with the aid of super-computers using and analysing the original voice patterns and re-creating them on other material? Maybe even on material that was written many years after the life of the artist in question. Although it may sound far-fetched, all sorts of mind-boggling innovations are being seen, as witness some recent TV commercials where footage of long-dead actors has been seamlessly integrated with that of extant ones. In the Third Millennium, it seems the camera most certainly *can* lie, and often does! Then there are the 'colorized' versions of old black-and-white films which have made an appearance in recent years (notably Presley's *Jailhouse Rock*, released in 1992). All of these technologies would have been impossible a few years ago — and who knows what's around the next corner?

- CHAPTER 4 -

Pickin' That Guitar

The happy afterthought

Back in 1935, around the time Elvis was born, the Holley family comprised father Lawrence Odell Holley, known as 'L.O.' (age 34), mother Ella (33), and their three children Larry (10), Travis (8) and daughter Pat (6). Both parents hailed from Texas, Drake being the maiden name of Buddy's mother. Their immediate ancestors were certainly American, although way back the line is said to have included English, Welsh and — as with Elvis — a touch of Cherokee Indian blood.

Whatever the ancestry, it must have come as a surprise in 1936 when the family, which to all intents and purposes had seemed complete, got ready to welcome an afterthought. The happy event took place (most appropriately) on 7 September — Labor Day — with mother and child both doing well, to use the time-honoured phrase. It seems the first that the other children knew of this little musical bundle was when they were taken into the bedroom to meet the new arrival and hear the decidedly unmusical sounds that greeted their ears! The new arrival was given the name Charles Hardin Holley*, although he quickly acquired the pet name of 'Buddy' and Charles was seldom if ever used.

As with Vernon Presley, Buddy's father Lawrence earned his living doing manual — if rather more skilled — work and held down a succession of jobs as diverse as carpenter, tailor and cook, frequently moving houses within the Lubbock County area as his family grew. Much of his spare time was taken up with church work and for a while he taught in Sunday School at the local Tabernacle Baptist Church where all the family worshipped. However, for the income needed to support the family, he eventually turned to tiling, helping his son Larry form the Lubbock Ceramic Tile Company in 1951 (it later became the Holley Tile Company) and remained involved in the venture from then on.**

Even though he 'couldn't carry a tune in a bucket' (to use his own phrase), he occasionally dabbled in the music business in a low-key kind of way, introducing Trini Lopez and his group, the Big Beats, to Norman Petty in 1957 after hearing them play on an army base in the Dallas area where he

---

* Hardin was an old family hand-me-down name and it was a pure coincidence that the unrelated Glen D. Hardin from Lubbock would later become a member of the Crickets. The latter also has a strong a link with Elvis Presley, as he was his musical arranger and keyboard player during the Seventies.

** Latest to join the trade is Buddy's niece, Sherry, who also specialises in both music and craftwork, presumably having inherited some of those same family genes.

Buddy's birthplace: 1911 6th Street, Lubbock. The house was dismantled and moved to an unknown destination shortly after this photograph was taken in 1977.

was working as a contractor. After Buddy's death, he helped Niki Sullivan launch his own group, the Hollyhawks.

As has already been noted, it wasn't at all unusual in those days for people to move house frequently and, of course, America has always had a reputation for its restless and shifting population, comprised as it is of a patchwork of migrants stretching back several hundred years. At the time Buddy put in his appearance, his family were living at 1911 6th Street, a small single-storey building where they remained for just one year. His birthplace these days is simply a vacant lot, albeit with a marker in place to draw attention to its historical significance.

The young Buddy Holly was a seemingly ordinary boy who — possibly because he came from a large family — was rather more gregarious than Elvis, even if to outsiders he could appear somewhat quiet and shy. It's a fact that many of his former teachers can't really remember much about him at all, but that's usually the way when teachers or employers are asked years later to recall someone famous from among their former charges. At that time, children didn't enter the education system until the advanced age of seven, so it must have been quite a relief to his parents when he eventually started school and could begin channelling some of the high energy which was beginning to make itself felt.

Buddy, in fact, spent periods at two different elementary schools because of house moves, eventually entering J.T. Hutchinson Junior High in 7th grade where he stayed until he graduated in 1955, two years later than

Wartime picture of the Holley family. Left to right: L.O., Buddy, Ella, Travis and Pat. Brother Larry is absent. Perhaps he took the photograph?

Elvis.[*] Academically speaking, neither was an outstanding student, and for Buddy music was one of the few possible — if remote — alternatives to the life of manual work that was beckoning. More than likely this would have meant labouring somewhere under a hot Texas sun, although he always had the option of going 'strawberry picking' (metaphorically speaking, that is) by joining his family in their tile business. But the picking that was driving him on was decidedly musical in nature, and with a lure that was to grow in intensity as the years unfolded.

Dual passions

Buddy may not have excelled academically, but he was certainly dextrous and artistic, and the schoolwork for which he is perhaps best remembered by those who knew him lay more on the vocational or hobby side of the divide. His early passions were in fact leatherwork and craftwork and, according to his erstwhile school chum Jerry Allison, he was very good at it too.

Buddy later made a decorated wallet for Marty Robbins, with whom he developed a friendship early on in his career, and also a pink-and-black

---

[*] Presley (who was born in January 1935) had entered the state school system in 1941, whereas Holly (born in September 1936 after the start of the academic year) was two years behind in school year terminology, entering the system in 1943.

Buddy aged seventeen
(from his 1954 High School Yearbook).

one for Elvis Presley which he delivered personally to the Sun studios while passing through Memphis. Whether it reached its intended recipient is not known, but it was a characteristically generous act by Buddy who remained a big fan of Elvis throughout his life.

More impressively still, Holly designed and hand-tooled a handsome leather cover for one of his own earliest acoustic guitars, a Gibson J-45 that was later acquired for almost a quarter of a million dollars by the actor Gary Busey, to whom we shall return later in connection with the *Buddy Holly Story* screen biography. As to the guitar, it's no coincidence at all that Elvis had flourished a similar hand-tooled Gibson with an ornate strap on one of his earliest performances in Lubbock, no doubt helping fire up Buddy in both of his passions.

As mentioned earlier, under the US system, Buddy didn't graduate until May 1955, by which time he was approaching nineteen and music had just about taken him over completely, even if he wasn't seeing the benefits yet in terms of dollar bills. He was certainly subsidised to a significant extent by his supportive parents during this period, and it's suggested that readers ignore the portrait of the family relationship as shown in the *Buddy Holly Story* biopic, which was wildly inaccurate according to everyone who knew the Holleys. (For example, the film depicts Buddy being berated by his parents for pursuing his love of rock & roll, and later embarrassing them in church one Sunday when his music is denounced from the pulpit. In actual fact, neither his parents nor his pastor were opposed to his activities, and he continued to tithe monies to his church until his passing.)

During his last two years at school, Buddy was in an Industrial Training Club and alongside some school studies such as American History he had employment of sorts with a couple of local companies — what we would probably term 'work experience' attachments nowadays. As his schooling drew to a close, music was beginning to intrude more and more, but it's worth putting those schooldays under scrutiny a tad more in view of what was to come after.

Unlike Elvis, who made his debut at school singing solo with just his guitar for accompaniment. Buddy really didn't show forth in that way, although he was part of an *a cappella* school choir called the Westernaires for a while. Photos of the ensemble depict him standing begowned and serious as one of a 35-strong group with nary a vocal solo or hiccup in evidence.* Even afterwards he didn't go down the solo route, but teamed up with classmate Bob Montgomery for the remainder of his schooldays. By this stage, both boys were already quite adept at the guitar and banjo (as is borne out by home recordings made at that time**) and pretty soon were performing together and attracting attention — even if at first it was for playing high school assemblies rather than paid gigs.

While the embryonic duo of Buddy & Bob was beginning to get noticed within the school precincts, a lucky development then occurred when Holly made the acquaintance of Jack Neal (a workmate of his father's) and hooked up with him to form Buddy & Jack. It's impossible to draw a sharp line between the two duos, as both were informal associations and it is known that they overlapped. Buddy, Bob and Jack would just get together as and when the gigs turned up and according to whoever was available at the time.

Neal (not to be confused with Gene Vincent's original bass player of the same name) was actually Buddy's senior by exactly two years and carpenter's mate to his dad, having moved north up Highway 87 from Takoma to live and work in the Lubbock area. Pretty soon, Buddy & Jack were a going concern, playing predominantly hillbilly with the occasional gospel number thrown in for good measure. Success followed quickly, with a regular spot on KDAV (reputedly the nation's first dedicated C&W station, known as 'K-Dave' after its founder 'Pappy' Dave Stone, who would later play a crucial role in getting Buddy his first recording contract) and even a few appearances on local TV. In November 1953, they recorded a couple of gospel numbers at the station — *I Hear The Lord Callin' For Me* and *I Saw The Moon Cry Last Night* — with Jack handling the vocal chores and Buddy playing guitar accompaniment.***

But, as with Elvis, it's impossible to pinpoint how a relatively unremarkable musically-inclined youth like Buddy Holly suddenly evolved into such a dynamic performer who would go on to carve out such a huge niche for himself in the short space of just eighteen months.

All those that hung around with Buddy in those early Lubbock days confirm that Elvis was his inspirational touchstone, but both men also

---

* Probably the most famous instance in pop/rock music of the hiccup (or, more correctly, glottal stop) used as a vocal device was Holly's memorable 'Well-uh-ell-uh-ell-uh-ell' introduction to *Rave On*.

** Much of their early work can be heard on the 1965 album, *Holly In The Hills*, which has yet to be reissued on CD. The 'duo' usually performed as a trio with Larry Welborn on bass, but were billed as 'Buddy & Bob' in line with other country music partnerships of the time (Homer & Jethro, Jim & Jesse, Johnnie & Jack, etc).

*** As these words are being typed, Rollercoaster Records in the UK are poised to release these recordings — fifty years after they were committed to acetate!

absorbed an enormous variety of influences that contributed to their musical development. The next chapter examines these in detail and may contain some surprises for those who haven't appreciated that rock & roll is both a many-layered and, in the words of the old song, a 'many-splendored thing'. If we want to get pretentious, let's briefly stand our corner and call it an art form. If longevity is a benchmark of worth, then few would argue to the contrary, even if the term 'rock & roll' itself has been hijacked and is nowadays indiscriminately applied — in the USA at least — to almost every other form of post-Fifties rock music.

Musical Interlude #4

(You're So Square) Baby I Don't Care **by Buddy Holly. Recorded at the Norman Petty Recording Studio, Clovis, New Mexico on 19 December 1957.**
The same title, recorded earlier by Elvis Presley at Radio Recorders Studio, Los Angeles on 3 May 1957.

Basically, there are seven songs* that Buddy Holly recorded which were also cut by Elvis, but only two of these — including the above track — were released during the Texan's lifetime.

Holly's version of *Baby I Don't Care* is an unashamed copy of the Presley recording except for the intriguing omission of the verse where Elvis sings 'you don't like hot-rod racing', at only one minute thirty-three seconds one of the briefest rock & roll recordings ever committed to wax.

Buddy had actually gone into the studio to cut three numbers to help make up the standard twelve tracks that were urgently required for his first solo album (at the time, *Peggy Sue* was shooting up the *Billboard* 'Top 100' towards its final resting place at No. 3, creating considerable demand for more of his material). Although long-playing albums had been around for several years, it was rare for a rock & roll singer to go into a studio in those days specifically to record an album, and contemporary LPs mostly consisted of a collection of an artist's singles with a few fillers added to round up the dozen.

Baby I Don't Care had originally been written for Elvis by the prolific

---

* This figure excludes snippets such as *Brown Eyed Handsome Man* which Elvis and others played around with during the 1956 'Million Dollar Quartet' session. Also worth noting is the fact that the seven Presley recordings were all studio masters, while most of the Holly versions were early demos or rehearsals and as such were not intended for release.

New York songwriting team of Jerry Leiber and Mike Stoller for the *Jailhouse Rock* film soundtrack that year. It wasn't released as a single either in the States or in Britain, but was included on the *Jailhouse Rock* EP, in which guise it got to No. 15 in the UK singles chart in 1958 and No. 14 in the newly-created EP chart three years later.

Holly's version was released on both sides of the Atlantic in 1958 on his solo *Buddy Holly* album, while a posthumous spin-off single reached No. 12 in the UK Top 20 in 1961 — a testament to his enduring popularity with the British audience.

The song lyrics themselves defy serious analysis, but are certainly an above-average example of the rock & roll genre circa 1957, being both witty and succinct.

Unusually, on the Elvis version, the singer played his own bass intro (Bill Black reportedly having thrown a tantrum and left the studio, later to be coaxed back for the remainder of the session).

Buddy certainly *didn't* attempt the bass part on his recording, which was handled as usual by Joe B. Mauldin — but drummer Jerry Allison got to play his part literally on the side of a cardboard box! A finer example of Fifties' musical improvisation it's probably harder to find unless it is Holly's manager, Norman Petty, playing water-filled wine glasses on *Oh You Beautiful Doll* (the flip of Jerry 'Ivan' Allison's 1958 solo hit, *Real Wild Child*), cut at those self-same studios in New Mexico.

Baby I Don't Care is seldom heard these days, although folk singer-songwriter Joni Mitchell scored a US Top 50 hit with it during 1982, while RCA finally put out Elvis' version as a single in the UK in 1983. It went to No. 61 — one of a long string of posthumous chart successes for the singer in the years immediately following his death.

- CHAPTER 5 -

Under The Influence

A musical patchwork

We now turn our thoughts in a different direction and take a look at the musical influences that Elvis Presley and Buddy Holly encountered in their formative years which helped to shape them and make them into what they were. How and where did they get to hear all the differing sounds and styles that helped to mould their music? Who were the heroes they looked up to from their similar Southern perspectives? What were the elements that each of them added to the brew that made their music so memorable?

The earliest influences on both men would inevitably been the sounds they heard around them while they were growing up: devotional music in church, popular music on the radio, classical music at school.

In Lubbock, the predominant style was decidedly hillbilly — epitomised by what was pumped over the airwaves from its Mecca at the *Grand Ole Opry* and in particular western swing, which had been born and bred a decade or two earlier deep in the heart of the Lone Star State itself. Although black influences were to play a major part in Buddy Holly's music, they would come along later. In contrast, although Elvis grew up much nearer to the accepted fount of country music than his counterpart, he also lived much closer to the black community and was exposed to the sounds of blues and gospel from a very early age.

Both boys also had a wide variety of recorded music all around them — not just on the radio, but also on jukeboxes and at home. This patchwork of influences would continue to be assimilated, utilised and adapted as they went along — deliberately in some instances, subconsciously in others.

Indeed, both later freely gave credit where it was due, although the quotes that exist are relatively few as neither man was ever subjected to the kind of in-depth interview that magazines such as *Rolling Stone*, *Playboy* and others of the genre cultivated in later years. Presley, of course, was permanently shielded from 1956 onwards by his autocratic manager, Colonel Tom Parker, while Holly prematurely 'left the building', to steal a quote.

The few insights we do have are nonetheless quite revealing. For example, in a rare early interview, Elvis admitted to admiring middle-of-the-road singers such as Bing Crosby, Dean Martin*, Billy Eckstine, the Ink Spots, Al Jolson, Patti Page and Kay Starr. He was also a fan of the classical tenor

---

* Martin recorded the original of *I Don't Care If The Sun Don't Shine* on Capitol in 1950, which Presley rocked up in 1954 for his second Sun single. In the event, however, it was songstress Patti Page who got the hit, charting No. 8 in 1950.

Balladeers Dean Martin, Patti Page and Al Jolson.

Mario Lanza (whom he later got to meet) and, from a bygone era, the legendary Enrico Caruso. In fact, it seems that, like Sinatra, Elvis loved the whole concept of *bel canto* — beautiful singer, beautiful song — though the term could hardly be applied to his early repertoire, which rarely included big ballads. But, if he suppressed this aspect in those early years in favour of a high-energy routine, he certainly gave full rein to it later in his career.

Conversely, there's nothing to suggest that Holly shared Presley's predilection for the ballad, the former coming into rock & roll from a strict western swing and bluegrass background coupled with a love of the black rhythms that he had started to discover. In fact, on his earliest professional recordings, he sounded quite ill at ease on some of the slower numbers, though by the time he cut *True Love Ways* and *Raining In My Heart* in October 1958, he seemed far more comfortable with the genre. Might his career have taken this direction had he lived longer? Perhaps the answer is to be found in his candid response to an interviewer who asked him whether he would change his style or continue to rock & roll: 'I'd hop on the trend!'

Country music

As has already been noted above, coming from the Deep South, both of our subjects had a background steeped in country & western music (or 'hillbilly' as it was still known in those days), even if Nashville didn't yet have the connotation or the influence within the music business that it has nowadays. Hillbilly was the music listened to by the white rural population throughout the South, and Elvis and Buddy could not have avoided it even if they tried.

Not that they did. Both later confessed to admiring Hank Snow (the 'Singing Ranger'), Bob Wills, the Louvin Brothers and the enigmatic Hank Williams, who not only sang the songs but also lived the wild life he portrayed in them.

Another of Elvis' earliest hillbilly heroes was the rather less well known Carvel Lee Ausborn *alias* Mississippi Slim, star of WELO, Tupelo, whom he reportedly 'followed round like a pet dog'. Indeed, at the age of ten or eleven, he appeared on the station's Saturday afternoon talent show, *Jamboree*, and sang two songs with his hero accompanying him on guitar — a double thrill that must surely have had a lasting impact on the youngster.

Country stars Hank Williams, Hank Snow and Eddy Arnold.

While Buddy undoubtedly also liked many of the artists that Elvis latched onto, there were also others who regularly passed through Texas such as Flatt & Scruggs, the Maddox Brothers & Rose and the home-grown Hank Thompson from Waco, who probably influenced him just as much as those listed above. Considering that he started off as a bluegrass picker, it's clear that Holly's country influences were rather different to those of Presley, who it is known was particularly attracted by the ballad-styled approach of Eddy Arnold.

Blessed with a significantly longer career, Elvis ended up recording many more country songs than Buddy, but it was the latter who actually performed more country music on the bandstand in the early Fifties, together with either Bob Montgomery or Jack Neal. In later years, we also learned that he occasionally also sat in with a popular local group, Ben Hall & The Ramblers[*], in the days before he first strapped on a Fender.

That Presley almost single-handedly helped to usher in a brash new form of music is surely without question, but this has to be coupled with the fact that his emergence virtually sounded the death knell for Tin Pan Alley and, as part of a double whammy, sidelined country music for a decade. Certainly during the Fifties and Sixties, the shifting music scene affected the earning capacity of many performers but — as with the old maxim — when one door closed, another creaked open and many country artists found themselves playing on rock & roll package shows or else appearing in one of the rash of black-and-white quickie movies that followed in the wake of the rock & roll explosion. (The real irony is that Presley and company had themselves originally been tacked on to country package shows before the reverse began to happen as rock & roll took over.) Elvis of course rose from the pack so quickly that, by the end of 1957, he had dispensed with package tours altogether although he continued to make guest appearances on the *Louisiana Hayride* and on many TV shows[**] until beckoned by Uncle Sam in 1958.

---

[*] Whilst they were never a household name outside of Texas, the Ramblers' pedal steel guitarist, Weldon Myrick, later became an indispensable Nashville session man.

[**] From late 1955 to 1958, he appeared on a succession of television shows, progressing from four appearances on Tommy and Jimmy Dorsey's poorly-rated *Stage Show* via Milton Berle and Steve Allen to the primetime *Ed Sullivan Show*. His first small screen appearance is rumoured to have been earlier — in October 1955 — as a guest of Roy Orbison and the Teen Kings on their weekly show on KOSA-TV, a small station in Odessa, Texas. This, however, remains unconfirmed.

R&B greats B.B. King, Roy Brown and Big Joe Turner.

Rhythm & blues

Another hugely important batch of influences for Elvis were the black singers and groups that he had always admired so much as he was growing up. As previously mentioned, interviews with the singer were scarce after the first couple of years, so not too much is documented under this heading. Despite this, it is known that he admired a whole host of rhythm and blues artists** including Big Bill Broonzy, Roy Hamilton, Ivory Joe Hunter, Lonnie Johnson (with whose *Tomorrow Night* he once serenaded his girlfriend Dixie), B.B. King, Little Milton, Muddy Waters, Lloyd Price, Arthur Prysock, Rufus Thomas and Joe Turner.

The magnitude of the influence is obvious from the choice of material for his first five singles — *That's All Right* (Arthur 'Big Boy' Crudup), *Good Rockin' Tonight* (Roy Brown), *Milkcow Blues Boogie* (Kokomo Arnold), *Baby Let's Play House* (Arthur Gunter) and *Mystery Train* (Little Junior Parker) — and from a host of later R&B covers including LaVern Baker's *Tweedlee Dee*, Ray Charles' *I Got A Woman* and *What'd I Say*, the Clovers' *Fool, Fool, Fool*, the Coasters' *Down In The Alley*, the Drifters' *Money Honey*, Billy Emerson's *When It Rains It Really Pours*, Little Richard's *Long Tall Sally* and *Tutti Frutti*, Lloyd Price's *Lawdy Miss Clawdy*, Joe Turner's *Shake, Rattle & Roll* and of course Big Mama Thornton's *Hound Dog*.

In direct contrast to Elvis, Buddy grew up in what was to all intents and purposes an all-white environment. There were black people in Lubbock, but they lived in another part of town and — unlike Memphis — rarely mingled with the white population. Whatever black influences Buddy absorbed would

---

*   It is noteworthy that both sides of his first demo were originally popularised by black artists: *My Happiness* was a 1948 R&B hit for Ella Fitzgerald as well as a pop hit for Jon & Sandra Steele; *That's When Your Heartaches Begin* was recorded in 1952 by the Ink Spots.

** A few years ago, Scotty Moore revealed that Elvis gave him a case of thirty or so of his 78s to transfer onto tape, and that of these twenty-four were by black artists — an amazingly high proportion. It's facts such as this that make it inconceivable that Elvis wasn't greatly influenced by blues and R&B. If further proof were needed, it could be added that he recorded six Ivory Joe Hunter compositions, and many more by other black writers — most notably the late Otis Blackwell (*alias* Charles Calhoun), whose talented pen provided him with monster hits like *Don't Be Cruel, All Shook Up, Return To Sender* and *One Broken Heart For Sale*.

Black talents Lloyd Price, Mahalia Jackson and Ivory Joe Hunter.

most likely have been via radio signals beamed into this rural part of Texas from out of state. Even if he himself was ring-fenced by the hillbilly music that the majority of his contemporaries favoured, he made certain that he got to hear as much of that 'other music' as he could — even if it meant having to stay up late at night with his friends to catch *Stan's Record Review* on KWKH, the 50,000-watt clear channel giant transmitting out of Shreveport, Louisiana, or sneak into the Cotton Club on 'colored' nights to see it in the flesh.

His favourites at the time included Tiny Bradshaw, Ray Charles, Fats Domino, Lightnin' Hopkins, Howlin' Wolf, Lonnie Johnson, B.B. King, Little Walter, the Midnighters and Muddy Waters. Not surprisingly, like Elvis, he went on to record many songs by black artists and composers including Chuck Berry's *Brown Eyed Handsome Man*, Roy Brown's *Good Rockin' Tonight*, Ray Charles' *Drown In My Own Tears*, the Clovers' *Ting-A-Ling*, Bo Diddley's *Bo Diddley* and *Mona*, Bill Doggett's *Honky Tonk*, Fats Domino's *Blue Monday* and *Valley Of Tears*, Arthur Gunter's *Baby Let's Play House*, Clarence 'Frogman' Henry's *Ain't Got No Home*, Little Richard's *Ready Teddy*, *Rip It Up* and *Slippin' & Slidin'*, Shorty Long's *Rock Me My Baby*, Mickey & Sylvia's *Dearest* and *Love Is Strange*, the Robins' *Smokey Joe's Cafe*, Joe Turner's *Shake, Rattle & Roll* and Chuck Willis' *It's Too Late*.

Gospel

If anything, gospel music had an even more profound influence on Elvis Presley than country music or R&B. Although he later expressed admiration for Mahalia Jackson, Clara Ward, Sister Rosetta Tharpe and other black gospel stars, as a teenager he was captivated by white quartets like the Blackwood Brothers and the Statesmen and regularly attended the monthly *All-Night Gospel Singings* held at the Ellis Auditorium in Memphis to experience first-hand the tremendous excitement they generated.

In *Last Train To Memphis*, Peter Guralnick concludes that 'gospel music combined the spiritual force that he felt in all music with the sense of physical release and exaltation for which, it seems, he was casting about.' Elvis himself put it more simply: 'It more or less puts your mind to rest.'

---

* Frustratingly, some of these recordings still have not been released.

The exuberant Statesmen, still going strong in the mid-Sixties.

Whatever, it is certainly no coincidence that he later surrounded himself with a permanent entourage of gospel-styled backing singers such as the Jordanaires, the Imperial Quartet (featuring Jake Hess), the Stamps (led by the impossibly deep-voiced J.D. Sumner) and Voice.

While Buddy Holly's involvement with gospel came nowhere near rivalling Presley's, it is nevertheless equally clear that he also loved the music (as he did almost all types of music that he encountered). In this context, it is particularly revealing to note that he based his *True Love Ways* on the old black gospel hymn, *I'll Be All Right* — perhaps after hearing the Angelic Gospel Singers' 1955 version on Nashboro.

Elvis Presley

Holly of course had one other major influence, and that was Elvis Presley himself, as he was always quick to point out. His heartfelt statement 'Without Elvis none of us could have made it' (taken from a 1957 interview shortly after his first big hit with the Crickets) says it all.

The feeling appears to have been mutual, too, though the only concrete evidence the author could trace was this quote from Roy Orbison: 'Elvis was a great admirer of Buddy, who he considered one of the true originals of rock & roll... Elvis had a complete collection of Buddy's records

---

* There are many other recordings of interviews where Holly cites Presley as his own major influence, as well as mentioning that he met up with him quite a few times in the early years.

and I can tell you he was pretty shook up when Buddy died so tragically.'

When he was up on stage, Presley was such a radically different performer to any seen before — certainly as far as white American audiences were concerned — that he completely blew away all those who witnessed his act. And it was most definitely the sudden appearance of Elvis treading the honky-tonk hardwood floors of Lubbock, Texas that whipped up all the influences that the young Buddy Holly had absorbed into a state of musical flux.

Later on in the Sixties, the Beatles' John Lennon was to put it even more simply: 'Before Elvis there was no-one.' (His other oft-quoted comment that 'Elvis died when he went into the army' possibly has no place in this book, but behind Lennon's caustic observation lies undeniable fact that the wholesome, safe, acceptable Elvis that emerged in 1960 was very different from the wild rebel who went in — a brilliant bit of rebranding by the astute Tom Parker.)

Popular culture

One other important factor that can't be overlooked where Elvis Presley is concerned is that some of his greatest early influences didn't come from any sort of musical background at all, but from the popular culture of the time.

As a child, he was an avid fan of the comic book superhero, Captain Marvel Junior, and later incorporated his lightning bolt motif into his renowned 'TCB' (Taking Care of Business) logo. The young Captain's glossy black hair unquestionably provided at least some of the inspiration for the famous Presley look, which also partially derived from the macho styles worn by long-distance truckers (sideburns, grease) and the sharp threads he saw blacks buying from Lansky's clothing store downtown.

The teenage Elvis was also enormously influenced by movies. He was a regular customer at the local fleapit and even worked as an usher for a while until he was fired following an altercation with a colleague. Always something of an outsider and a loner, it is easy to understand why he felt an immediate empathy with the alienated, sensitive, misunderstood anti-hero portrayed by Tony Curtis in 1949's *City Across The River*, and later with James Dean's desperate character in *Rebel Without A Cause*.

One of the great mysteries about Presley's meteoric rise to stardom is how he managed to transform himself from a painfully shy, bumbling nineteen year old into the dynamic 'Hillbilly Cat' of legend within the short space of one year. Perhaps the answer lies here.

There's little doubt that he had been spellbound by the stars he saw up there on the silver screen during those impressionable years. It seems he felt that, while the world of film provided escapism for the masses, it might also one day also provide him with a means of escape from a life of poverty in Memphis, possibly even the chance to make something of himself. If historically we've got used to actors who really wanted to be singers, there is the distinct suspicion with Elvis that in his case the converse was true. Tony Curtis, Marlon Brando, Richard Widmark, James Dean and later Yul Brynner

Messrs. Dean and Presley model the popular mid-Fifties 'surly' look.

were all idols of his, as was that tragic silent screen figure from the past, Rudolph Valentino (1895–1926).

What we *do* know is that Elvis desperately wanted to get into films and, although in later years it has always been fashionable to state that his role as a film star was a natural progression from his career in music, there was certainly more to it than that. Of course, part of the equation was the cynical Colonel Tom Parker, who it seems got him his first big Hollywood break and thereafter forever tried to milk even bigger bucks out of his boy whilst exhibiting a total disregard for the quality of the end product.

Sadly, Elvis found himself trapped in a corner for most of his career and seemed powerless to break out and go after the kind of film roles he initially coveted. That it was a matter of bitter disappointment to him can't be overestimated, and the fact that his screen career started so promisingly only to nosedive in the Sixties must have been a shattering blow to his pride and his hidden ambitions. Were even his fantastic achievements as a recording artist really sufficient compensation one wonders?

We've been hovering near 1955 for far too long, so now is as good a point as any to break off and examine that year and challenge Elvis by saying: 'Elvis, you *did* meet Buddy Holly in Lubbock, even if the name and the voice seemed unfamiliar, and it was all so hectic back then that you couldn't quite match the denim-clad young hopeful with the polished act you saw on TV in 1958 on the *Ed Sullivan Show*. Let's take you back and see if you remember after all. I think you will.'

Musical Interlude #5

Valley of Tears by Buddy Holly. Recorded at the Norman Petty Recording Studio in Clovis, New Mexico circa May–July 1957.

One Night by Elvis Presley. Hit version recorded February 1957 at Radio Recorders Studio, Los Angeles.

The common link between these two recordings is Fats Domino, the great rhythm & blues singer/pianist who both artists openly admired as one of the major contributors to the new sound of rock & roll in the mid-Fifties.

Valley of Tears was a big hit for Domino in both the UK and the US in 1957, and was co-composed by Fats and his musical partner, Dave Bartholomew. The song was a particular favourite of Larry Holley, who suggested to his brother that he should record it for future release, and it subsequently appeared in 1958 on his solo LP, *Buddy Holly*. Released on a single in the UK as the flip of *Baby I Don't Care*, it became a double-sided hit in 1961, reaching No. 12 in the Top Twenty.

Much of the attraction in Holly's version of the Domino song is the prominent 'church organ' accompaniment played by Norman Petty. Sadly, Buddy didn't get the chance to record any hymns or gospel material in his brief career, so this and *Early In The Morning* are probably as close as we get to imagining how he might have sounded had he got the opportunity.

By comparison, Presley's song (also coincidentally part-written by Dave Bartholomew) is a much earthier performance, having originally been a R&B hit in 1956 for another New Orleanian, Smiley Lewis, labelmate and contemporary of Fats Domino. The original version as sung by Lewis was entitled *One Night (Of Sin)* and was certainly not intended for the ears of white middle-class audiences, let alone those of their impressionable offspring.

Consequently, both title and lyrics were rewritten for Elvis' recording, although no-one was more frustrated than the singer that such sanitisation was deemed necessary. Released in October 1957, the cleaned-up version became a No. 4 *Billboard* 'Top 100' smash in March 1958. Interestingly enough, it subsequently transpired (when RCA released it several years after his death) that he had in fact originally recorded the number in its full unexpurgated glory a month or so earlier.

- CHAPTER 6 -

A Musical Tornado Hits Lubbock!

Life in the Texas Panhandle

In Lubbock, Texas, a dozen fair-sized tornados hit town each year, but during 1955 this figure was knocked sideways as, on at least a further five occasions, a musical whirlwind in the guise of Elvis Presley arrived to upset the average. The first of these occurred before the new year had hardly got underway, while the last was in October, by which time Presley's fame had grown to the extent that the following year was to be far and away the most successful of his life, period. 1956 would be a magical twelve-month for Elvis, when he carried all before him with scarcely a backward glance or pelvic twitch — that's if we discount the damp squib of his first Vegas debut that April, his only real setback.

In fact, it was the unsuspecting locals of Lubbock who saw him perform in 1955 that were amongst the first to bear witness to a dynamic, vibrant, *sexy* new phenomenon who not only touched the heart-strings of all those females present, but whose bravado and showmanship also appealed to the male segment of the audience — particularly if like Buddy Holly or Sonny Curtis you were striving to be a musician!

Elvis had first started playing such one-nighters as early as July 1954 on tours that gradually moved outward from Memphis and neighbouring Tennessee, but it wasn't until 1955 had rolled around that Lubbock began to figure in his itinerary. The city at that moment became the most distant point that he had yet travelled to, with the sole exception of Odessa — 140 miles due south on Highway 62 — where his trio had made their debut just before Christmas 1954.

Although dwarfed by large metropolitan areas such as Dallas and Houston, Lubbock today has a population approaching 200,000, having been a regional centre for music in West Texas for many years — an influence that continues to grow. We probably have to go right back to Bob Wills & His Texas Playboys or Milton Brown & His Musical Brownies to begin tracing the many and varied musicians who are associated with West Texas, and the link continues through the Maines Brothers Band and Mac Davis to the present day, with Joe Ely and most recently the Dixie Chicks making a continuing contribution to the music of the region.

While Lubbock couldn't compete with the Dallas Sportatorium, which hosted KRLD's *Big D Jamboree* for years, or the *Louisiana Hayride* just over the border in Shreveport, it was nevertheless an important stopping-off point situated as it is at the base of the Texas Panhandle. In the Fifties, the five thousand-seater Fair Park Coliseum was the premier auditorium in the city

Buddy, Larry and Bob snapped at the KDAV studio circa February/March 1955.

from the moment it opened its doors in October 1954 and was able to stage large jamboree-style shows that could challenge most others around the South. It was certainly in a different league from the city's smaller, more dubious venues such as the Cotton Club* or the Bamboo Club, and the rather more innocent Lawson Roller Rink (which was recreated so effectively in the 1978 *Buddy Holly Story* biopic).

Let's transport ourselves back now to 1955, look at each concert in detail and piece together as much of the relevant information as possible to see how the lives of Elvis Presley and Buddy Holly first brushed up against each other during that year.

We've already noted that Elvis, with hits in the local Memphis charts, was much further forward in career terms than Buddy, who as an unpaid amateur remained very much the 'unappreciated musician'. Presley was already a professional performer, even if he was still unknown outside the confines of nearby states. Holly, on the other hand, was totally unknown outside of West Texas, although he had received occasional fan letters from listeners in New Mexico following his regular appearances with Bob

---

* The Cotton Club was a late-night venue, and it's highly probable that Elvis performed there after most if not all of his Fair Park shows. Unfortunately, while those latter appearances are well documented by way of press reports and advertisements, those at the Cotton Club are not. The original club building burned down in the early 1960s.

Montgomery and Larry Welborn on KDAV's *Sunday Party*. Indeed, by the end of 1954 the 'Buddy & Bob Show' segment had become so popular that kids would drive out to the station to watch the performers through the window while listening to the broadcast on their car radios!

But just what was mid-Fifties Lubbock like, bearing in mind that there aren't many corners of the globe that have remained unchanged over the past half-century? Well, the intimidating fact then and now is that you can drive into Texas at daybreak starting from Oklahoma in the north, pass through Lubbock towards the base of the Panhandle and come dusk you will still be driving within the state border, such is the vastness of the land there. The complete diagonal taken to arrive at the Mexican border would encompass over 750 miles as the Texan crow (or should that be buzzard?) flies.

To the British visitor, the journey would even be significantly further than the time-honoured domestic one from Lands End to John O'Groats, which these days seems to be reserved primarily for charity walkers and cyclists. Along the way, the giant vistas of Texas would be markedly different to the familiar 'green and pleasant' rural landscapes of Great Britain. For example, in several parts of the Lone Star State, it is possible to travel hundreds of miles without ever seeing a tree or even a bush! But if everything Texan is different, or just plain big and intimidating, maybe that's part of the attraction for anyone visiting this border state, which didn't even become part of the Union until 1845.

Lubbockites themselves seem pretty laid-back individuals who cope with the dominating landscape and extreme weather patterns with a markedly taciturn outlook. Not too much bothers them now and it certainly didn't back then, although things got slightly ruffled back in the mid-Fifties when Elvis hit town and caused that conservative façade to briefly buckle!

To fully appreciate what went down, we need to take an even closer look at the history of this part of Texas back to the earliest days when Lubbock was founded. That was in 1891, when rival groups of entrepreneurs who had recently established settlements to the north and south of Yellow House Canyon (old Lubbock and Monterey respectively) came together in a rare spirit of enterprise and cooperation and agreed to dismantle and move both towns to a new site to create the present-day Lubbock (named, like the county in which it stands, after Tom S. Lubbock, a former Texas Ranger, Confederate officer and brother of Francis R. Lubbock, Civil War governor of the state of Texas).

Back then, cattle ranching was the predominant activity in the area and the wide open terrain was inhabited by a population numbering barely more than a thousand. It wasn't until cotton became established at the turn of the century that strong regional growth took place and Lubbock began to gain prominence. Nowadays, within a radius of one hundred miles of the city, two million cotton bales are produced annually, Lubbock County alone contributing a quarter of a million towards that total. Small wonder that the slogan adorning local billboards is *'Cotton is cool, Cotton is healthy, Cotton is nature'*!

The way in which the city has expanded over the years can be dramatically illustrated by comparing estimated population numbers using Buddy Holly's life as a template: when he was born in the Thirties, the population was around 25,000, but by 1955 that figure had reached 116,000; by the time of his death in 1959, it had risen to approximately 130,000. Today that figure can be increased by half again, with the total population of the city rapidly pushing towards the 200,000 mark.

A church town from its inception — it was originally settled predominantly by Quakers and two Church of Christ groups — Lubbock was quick to found schools, colleges, clubs and societies (both religious and non-religious) which contributed greatly to its development as a metropolis.

Not surprisingly, music played a central role in the lives of many early Lubbockites, both in church and at social functions like the popular weekend picnics which would usually end with a square dance: if nothing else, it provided a welcome diversion from the unremitting endlessness of the surrounding countryside. The original Lubbock Band — usually consisting of two violins, three guitars and a double bass — regularly played at these affairs, later moving to a purpose-built bandstand in the central square around which the town was built.

As the city grew, so did its nightlife, and by the 1930s Lubbock — in common with many other small towns and cities in the area — was hosting live Saturday-night 'jamborees' featuring local hillbilly talent. Situated three hundred miles or so from the nearest large conurbation, the city often also found itself in the fortunate position of playing host to out-of-town acts who would ordinarily have played much bigger places. In the mid-Fifties, these would have included country singers like Webb Pierce, Faron Young or Hank Snow — all listed as the biggest sellers in their field during 1954. But things were now about to change in a most dramatic way.

1st visit: Thursday, 6 January 1955 at the Fair Park Coliseum

Right at the very outset of this list of visits that Elvis Presley made to Lubbock during 1955, it must be conceded that there may be some room for error as to the exact dates and venues involved. As everyone knows, Elvis broke through nationally (and internationally) in 1956 with *Heartbreak Hotel*, and his life was put under a microscope from then on. However, the period immediately preceding this was — and still is — largely ignored, falling as it did outside of his main years of fame and fortune. Back then, there was also the strong possibility that this new-fangled 'rock & roll' music would be a short-lived phenomenon and would evaporate just as quickly as it had arrived. Most fans would have received a very small trickle of information in those days, and probably had to content themselves with press releases or what they heard over the radio and TV as the controversy of those early appearances unfolded week by week. It was only gradually, over a lengthy period, that individuals emerged from all over who were sufficiently fascinated by the music and its heroes to try and unravel some of the mystery of just how rock & roll and Elvis had evolved.

As to this initial Lubbock visit, it almost certainly took place on 6 January — the first Thursday of the New Year — and that's the date favoured both by the respected Holly historian John Ingman and also Lee Cotten, author of several Presley-related books including *Did Elvis Sing In Your Hometown?* Conversely, Sonny Curtis (who was also on the bill that day) thinks Sunday the 2nd was more likely, as he recalls the appearance as coming just after the holiday season. However, by piecing together where Elvis was before and after, Thursday the 6th emerges as the more probable of the two.

Whatever the actual date, we do know that just before (on New Year's Day 1955), Bob Neal signed a contract to become his sole manager — a situation that would not obtain for long, as a certain counterfeit Colonel was waiting in the wings getting ready to muscle in. This he would achieve by gradually squeezing Neal out of the frame in the ensuing months, finally taking over completely during 1956.

The uncertainties about dates and managers aside, the venue for Elvis Presley's first appearance in Lubbock was most definitely the aforementioned Fair Park Coliseum, a spacious covered auditorium in the city's Fair Grounds district which had opened the previous October. It would thereafter play host to most of the big country acts that passed through on a regular basis.

IN PERSON

Elvis
PRESLEY
SCOTTY and BILL

"That's All Right Mama"
"Blue Moon of Kentucky"
"Good Rockin Tonite"
Heartbreaker"

FUN! MUSIC! JOKES!

The prestigious Fair Park shows were usually arranged under the auspices of one or other of the local radio stations, and so it was with Elvis' debut too. Local radio personality William 'Hipockets' Duncan (who coincidentally also acted as Buddy Holly's manager up until he signed with Decca in 1956) and the previously-mentioned 'Pappy' Dave Stone of KDAV were the promoters of the show, which featured the Memphian on a country bill alongside local lad Sonny Curtis, Jimmy & Johnny (who'd had a big hit the previous year with *If You Don't Somebody Else Will*), comedian Peach Seed Jones and headliner Billy Walker from Ralls, Texas — a pretty big name back then down South thanks to his numerous appearances on the *Louisiana Hayride* and *Big D Jamboree*, and the local success of his recent Columbia release, *Thank You For Calling*. Sadly, no posters from this show have survived to flesh out the minor members of the bill — such as the tantalizing (albeit remote) possibility that a youthful Roy Orbison from nearby Wink may also have been one of the attractions!

Just picture the scene as Elvis, Scotty and Bill rolled into Lubbock packed inside Scotty's 1954 yellow Chevrolet Bel-Air together with all their musical gear in those pre-roadie days. If that doesn't sound too much of a problem, remember that the instruments would have included one rather large double-bass strapped to the car roof!

Although Billy Walker was officially the star of the show, it was Presley — with two Sun singles already under his belt, but still without a national hit record — who pulverised the audience that evening. The comments of Sonny Curtis eloquently describe the tremendous impact he created as he strode onto the stage flanked by Scotty and Bill: 'He had on an orange sports coat, red pants, white bucks. Tell you what boy, he looked like a motorsickle headlight *[that's Texan speak!]* comin' right at you!'

Curtis remembers being particularly impressed with the effect the singer had on the ladies in the audience: 'I wanted to be just like him — or as close as I could get. It was the "girl factor" that intrigued me!'

The music too, left his public mesmerised: ten, maybe a dozen songs including frantic versions of his Sun singles — his third, *Milkcow Blues Boogie* b/w *You're A Heartbreaker*, came out later that week — mixed in with R&B rockers like *Good Rockin' Tonight*, *Tweedlee Dee*, *Shake, Rattle & Roll* and *Fool, Fool, Fool*[*]. Think of this if you will: from taking the stage to taking a bow, Elvis probably played for little more than thirty frenetic minutes. But wouldn't you just love to have been there?

If there had ever been any doubt on that cool Texan night, a sea change in popular culture was witnessed in the making as venue after venue fell under the spell of Elvis Presley and his fame rippled outwards (or more specifically, northwards) to the rest of the United States.

From that moment on, Buddy decided that he would have to form a trio based on the Elvis, Scotty and Bill model, even if it meant for the moment passing his beloved Fender Stratocaster over to Sonny Curtis so that he could take centre stage with Sonny's D-28 Martin acoustic. He'd need to change his vocal style too, abandoning those drawn-out nasal country tones in favour of a more urgent, breathy delivery cranked up to emulate the Presley style. To paraphrase John Lennon, who when speaking about his early influences once explained that he 'was' Buddy Holly for a time, from early January 1955 Buddy 'was' Elvis Presley!

Although Buddy was totally knocked out with Presley's wild music and dynamic showmanship, and doubtless watched the proceedings slack-jawed, it seems frustratingly likely he didn't get to speak to him on this occasion. Fortunately, Elvis was to return to Lubbock for another show just over a month later. This time things were rather different, as Buddy not only got to meet up with his idol backstage, but was also on the bill that day.

---

[*] While this list is naturally speculative, two live radio recordings of Presley performing in Lubbock around that time have surfaced. These songs — covers of the Clovers' *Fool, Fool, Fool* and Joe Turner's *Shake, Rattle & Roll* — were released in 1992 on the *Complete Fifties Masters* box set. It is known that they date from either his first or second appearance, but unfortunately no other information is to hand.

Elvis mobbed by fans in Lubbock. This picture is thought to date from his first visit. Larry Welborn is immediately behind Elvis; Buddy and Bob are on the extreme far right.

2nd visit: Sunday, 13 February 1955 at the Fair Park Coliseum

Five weeks after his first appearance, Elvis was back in Lubbock by popular demand — this time as the headliner of a one-off *'Matinee'* performance starting at four o'clock. Just the day before, he had joined the *Hank Snow Jamboree* in Carlsbad, New Mexico, courtesy of Hank's manager — a certain Colonel Tom Parker — and the tour would continue on to Roswell, New Mexico on 14 February before heading eastwards towards Memphis. The one thing that is certain is that days and nights were hectic for Elvis, who most likely also shoehorned in a late-night show at Lubbock's Cotton Club that same evening.*

The set that Elvis performed that night probably varied little from his January show, although it would doubtless have included his rocked-up version of Arthur Gunter's recent regional R&B hit, *Baby Let's Play House***, which he was to record at Sun later that month for his fourth single (released in April 1955).

---

* Although this is unconfirmed, it does seem to have been routine for many artists apart from the main headliners to play both venues on the same day, the Fair Park shows being afternoon or early evening whilst the Cotton Club, only a few miles away, was a late-night establishment.

** Having seen Elvis perform the song, Buddy cut a demo of it in the summer of 1955, coming closer to approximating the Sun sound than with any other record of his career. It was one of several demos he cut at the Nesman studios in Wichita Falls that year as part of his continuing efforts to get a record deal.

The rest of this *Big Western Show* ('Western' was the traditional term most used then) comprised the following artists and is representative of many similar bills of the time: Whitey Ford, who specialised in country humour and went by the quaint title of the 'Duke of Paducah'; Jimmie Rodgers Snow, son of Hank Snow, who sang country music (and later some rock & roll) before taking Holy Orders and denouncing the music as sinful; a rocking lady by the name of Charlene Arthur who never got the big break, although she probably helped to pave the way for Brenda Lee, Wanda Jackson and others; singer/guitarist Ace Ball, who was a big local act at this time and had several releases on West Texas labels throughout the Fifties; Bill Myrick & The Rainbow Riders, a popular act from nearby Odessa; and opening the bill, those hometown boys, Buddy & Bob, with their friend Larry Welborn again sitting in on bass. Inspired by Elvis, their business card now stated that they performed *'Western and Bop'* music! Things were already moving.

It is also known that, in the brief period between Presley's two appearances, Buddy & Bob filed their first composition, *I Just Don't Care*, with music publishers Ridge Way Music on 5 February 1955, although what became of this song and whether it was a country ballad or a rocker is uncertain. The title appears to reflect country sensibilities, but equally it may have been an attempt at rockabilly (like *Down The Line*, another of their early compositions).

Indeed, by this time, Buddy was beginning to lean increasingly towards rock & roll — much to Bob Montgomery's distaste. He would leave at the end of the year to work for producer Norman Petty in Clovis, New Mexico, and later moved to Nashville for a lengthy career in country music during which he has only made the occasional foray into pop.

Someone else who also enters the frame — either on this occasion or upon Elvis' next visit to Lubbock in April — is future country superstar Waylon Jennings. Jennings, from nearby Littlefield, was one of many local talents who would later pass through the Crickets' ranks and in fact accompanied Buddy on his final tour.

Back then, however, he was simply an aspiring musician just like Buddy, whom he'd met around 1953–54 when the latter first started appearing on KDAV's *Sunday Party*. Soon after, Jennings — at the tender age of seventeen — landed a job as deejay on local station KLLL (or 'K-triple-L' as the catchy call-sign went) and never looked back.

In his autobiography, *Waylon*, the singer describes Elvis visiting Lubbock on a bill which starred Hank Snow and Martha Carson[*], but whether he caught all of Elvis' appearances in Lubbock is unclear. It's probably pure guesswork, but Jennings mentions that the first time he played Lubbock the booking fee was only $50, while by the year end the price had shot up to $4,000![**] Be that as it may, it's a fact that Presley gradually began to

---

[*] Presley never played Lubbock on a bill that included both Hank Snow and Martha Carson. Jennings appears to have confused his third gig (headlined by Snow) with his fourth (which featured Carson).

[**] It was reported at the time that Presley was paid $75 for his second (13 February 1955) appearance, and $4,000 for a show on 10 April 1956, so the figures appear to be roughly correct.

BY POPULAR DEMAND

ELVIS
PRESLEY

The Be-Bop Western Star of the L.A. Hayride Returns to Lubbock.

4:00 P.M. MATINEE
TODAY ONLY
FAIR PARK COLISEUM

ALSO ON THE BIG WESTERN SHOW:

DUKE OF PADUCAH—of the Grand Ole Opry "Get On The Wagon, Boys, These Shoes Are Killing Me."

CHARLENE ARTHUR—Miss Dynamite of the Big D Jamboree and Victor Records.

JIMMIE RODGERS SNOW—Son of Hank Snow and Victor Recording Artist

ACE BALL—Okeh Recording Artist

BILL MYRICK and the **RAINBOW-RIDERS**

BUDDY AND BOB

BOXOFFICE OPENS AT 2:30

command bigger fees as the year progressed and his regional fame continued to spread outwards. It's also certain that, of all the territories where he was initially popular, West Texas was probably the hottest of the lot for Elvis back in the spring of '55.

So, without further speculation, let's put that third Lubbock visit under the microscope and examine his increasing impact on the area — not only on his rapidly-growing audiences, but also on a whole gang of relatively unknown young local musicians in that corner of the Lone Star State including Jennings, Sonny Curtis, Jerry Allison, Buddy Knox, Jimmy Bowen, Roy Orbison, Terry Noland and, of course, a certain Charles Hardin Holley. Many other names will probably never be known except to the real devotees of the music as they 'forked no lightning', even if lots of the real stuff was forever overhead in the sweltering Texas night air.

3rd visit: Friday, 29 April 1955 at the Cotton Club

To help make sense of the musical timeframe we are in, we need to mention the period between the last February visit and this one at the end of April. The gap between Elvis Presley's first two visits to Lubbock had been only five weeks; this time it was twice as long. However, he had been anything but idle, having played continuously throughout the Deep South either on short tours with the likes of Hank Snow or Billy Walker, or else on a stream of one-nighters.

In between, he had squeezed in a flight to New York during March in a failed attempt to get national exposure via a spot on the popular *Arthur Godfrey's Talent Scouts* TV show. In hindsight, it may seem ludicrous that Elvis Presley of all people should fail such an audition, but fail to impress he did, and the show that gave Steve Lawrence, Julius LaRosa, Pat Boone and

Guy Mitchell their big break decided to pass on Elvis.* What that fact does reinforce is that, in addition to his wild music, Presley's dress and physical appearance in 1955 were so different to the conventions of the day and so outrageous to the older generation that he struggled to win many people over the first time around. So, as with his disastrous first *Grand Ole Opry* appearance, the Hillbilly Cat was again rocked back onto the heels of his pedal-pushers and for a while longer it seemed a frustrating possibility that he might never break out beyond the confines of the Mason-Dixon Line to the larger audience that his talent so obviously deserved.

Looking back, this must have been an immensely frustrating period in his life, despite the fact that he was destroying audiences wherever he played. Would he ever break out beyond the borders of a cluster of Southern states or just continue to tour the same backwater towns over and over again?

Another reason for his frustration was that, for some time now in the liberal North, the old social barriers had been coming down making it possible for white performers like Johnnie Ray to appear on the same bills as black artists — something that would not have happened in less enlightened times, and certainly not down South. By the mid-Fifties, Alan Freed and others were regularly promoting R&B spectaculars featuring the likes of Joe Turner, Fats Domino, the Clovers and

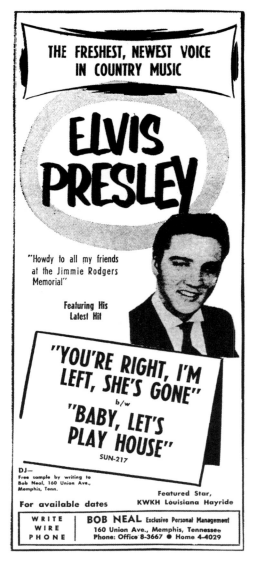

THE FRESHEST, NEWEST VOICE IN COUNTRY MUSIC

ELVIS PRESLEY

"Howdy to all my friends at the Jimmie Rodgers Memorial"

Featuring His Latest Hit

"YOU'RE RIGHT, I'M LEFT, SHE'S GONE"
b/w
"BABY, LET'S PLAY HOUSE"
SUN-217

DJ—
Free sample by writing to
Bob Neal, 160 Union Ave.,
Memphis, Tenn.

For available dates

Featured Star,
KWKH Louisiana Hayride

WRITE WIRE PHONE	BOB NEAL Exclusive Personal Management 160 Union Ave., Memphis, Tennessee Phone: Office 8-3667 ● Home 4-4029

---

* A similar fate befell the Crickets in May 1957, only they never even made it to the Big Apple. The group auditioned in Amarillo, Texas (a hundred miles or so north of Lubbock), where Jerry Allison recalls them tackling a pounding Little Richard rocker and some of their own material and noticeably failing to sway the ultra-conservative show's local representatives. Like Elvis, the Crickets were also on the verge of success. (In marked contrast, the Johnny Burnette Rock'n'Roll Trio — one of the wildest of all the early rockabilly groups — cleaned up in 1956, winning a rival talent show, *Ted Mack's Original Amateur Hour*, three times in a row. Ironically, they subsequently failed to score any national hits.)

Etta James and selling out big venues in New York and other major cities. National exposure was at last within reach for many black acts, even if, for now, cover versions by white acts like Bill Haley, Pat Boone and others creamed off the major record sales.

Stuck in a rut down South, Elvis — Sam Phillips' 'white boy who could sing like a negro' — was simply unable to connect with where the action was. It must have increasingly seemed to him that he would have to content himself with being a big fish in the proverbial small pool — not a scenario that fitted in with his dreams of stardom. Having hits on the Memphis chart certainly meant he was selling thousands of records — excellent figures in regional Tennessee terms, but mere drops in the ocean when compared with the million-sellers being racked up increasingly by a burgeoning group of proto-rock & rollers.

Whether such thoughts were going through his mind as he played the Cotton Club that night is not known, but his fourth single (*I'm Left, You're Right, She's Gone* b/w *Baby Let's Play House*) had just come out and things would very soon begin to take off for him in a big way.

Lubbock's Cotton Club, of course, bore no relation to the legendary New York niterie that was the Mecca for most of the jazz world from the late Twenties onwards. This version (like many other 'Cotton Clubs' across the South) was an unsophisticated establishment housed in a converted quonset hut — certainly much smaller and less salubrious than the grand Fair Park Coliseum where Elvis had appeared on his two previous visits.

Although Lubbock itself was 'dry' until 1978, the Cotton was permitted to operate as a 'bottle club' where patrons brought and consumed their own alcohol — a practice known as 'set-ups'. However, on *Teen Night* (a weekly show for teenagers, such as those on which Elvis appeared), only soft drinks were allowed.

The decor was simple, with huge bales of cotton strategically placed around the stage to separate the crowd from the performers. Unlike the auditorium at Fair Park, it also included a dance floor which doubtless occasionally doubled as a wrestling ring when things livened up. Well-known local personality Slim Corbin mostly fronted the house band, but quite a few name acts also appeared there when they passed through town.

At the time, Elvis was between tours, waiting to embark on his biggest to date — the *Hank Snow All Star Jamboree* — which was due to commence on Sunday, 1 May in New Orleans and run across the length and breadth of the South for three months. As if having Hank and Elvis on the same bill wasn't enough, the remaining list of acts for the upcoming tour reads like a *Who's Who* of Fifties' country music talent: Faron Young, the Wilburn Brothers, Mother Maybelle and the Carter Sisters, the Davis Sisters (one of whom was Skeeter Davis), Onie Wheeler, and once again Jimmie Rodgers Snow. (It was reportedly a matter of considerable frustration to Elvis that the latter was signed by RCA a year before he was.)

And so it came to pass that Elvis sneaked into Lubbock's Cotton Club on the Friday evening of 29 April to play a show which again would find Buddy Holly in the audience, determined not to miss the musical shaman who had had such an overwhelming impact on his life. (Also on the bill that night were Gene Kay, Chuck Lee and Capitol recording artist Dub Dickerson.)

Whilst the playlist for Presley's show would have been pretty much as before and most likely included most of his Sun single sides, he was now also beginning to feature more R&B numbers, which suited his high energy stage act. Of these, LaVern Baker's *Tweedlee Dee* remained a favourite and was included in his set (as it would be the following evening when he appeared on a *Louisiana Hayride* remote broadcast* from Gladewater, just east of Dallas, close to the Louisiana border).

Things were slowly starting to move for Buddy too, although he was to experience several setbacks before he finally got a foothold on that slippery ladder of success. One of these is described below and it is probably fair to say that, if Elvis was finding regional popularity and several mildly successful records a source of disappointment, Buddy would have settled for getting a darned audition at this point!

It's hard to pinpoint just exactly when this setback occurred. It may well have been just after this particular Cotton Club show, although the few snippets of information on the subject are inconsistent. Whatever the date, it seems that Elvis advised him that he should try to get onto the *Louisiana Hayride* radio show as a first step to stardom. In Buddy's mind that was all the encouragement he needed and, once the logistics had been worked out, he drove the five hundred miles to Shreveport with Bob Montgomery and Larry Welborn. The optimistic thinking was that they would just knock on the door and say: 'Here we are! Elvis sent us.'

Maybe that was the dream, and maybe on another day it might have worked exactly like that, but fate decreed that their hero would be out of town and the three young Texan hopefuls didn't even manage to get past the front desk. And so, the boys had a long, sad drive back to Lubbock with their instruments, having clocked up a daunting and wholly unproductive one thousand miles in the process.

Before they could get too discouraged, however, the Tupelo Tornado was back in town and Buddy's disappointment quickly subsided as he once again experienced an object lesson in how to tear up an audience.

4th visit: Friday, 3 June 1955 at the Johnson-Connelly Pontiac showroom, Fair Park Coliseum and the Cotton Club

Barely a month elapsed before Elvis was back on Buddy's home turf and, as with the previous appearance at the Fair Park auditorium in February, Buddy again found himself opening the show for him.

In an advertised one-off personal appearance at 7:00 pm earlier that evening, Elvis had turned up to open a new Pontiac showroom situated at the intersection of Main Street and Avenue Q. There he signed autographs but, sadly for the crowds in attendance, didn't get to perform. Buddy (who was by now quite well known locally) also went along, but an educated guess would be that the Lubbockites stood in a longer line to get napkins or whatever

---

* A 'remote' was the term in those days for a live broadcast from a concert location rather than from within the studio.

signed by Elvis than they did for their own man. One thing is certain: it must have been a fleeting appearance for both of them, as the curtain was due to go up at 8:00 pm for the show way across town.

Once again, the event was sponsored by KDAV's 'Pappy' Dave Stone and Hipockets Duncan, and this time around Elvis was most emphatically the headliner. Advertised as a *'Combination Grand Ole Opry–Louisiana Hayride Show'*, the bill was a star-studded one in country music terms, with Ferlin Husky, the Carlisles, Martha Carson, Jim Ed & Maxine Brown, Onie Wheeler, George & Earl (*Got Anything Good, Goin' Steady With The Blues*), the Country Gentlemen and Lubbock's own Buddy & Bob (and Larry) — all for an eminently reasonable $1 entrance fee.

Holly had, in fact, only graduated from High School one week earlier at a formal ceremony that, coincidentally, was also held at Lubbock's premier venue — that very same Fair Park Coliseum! How weird must that have been for him: one week standing there be-gowned and serious to receive his graduation scroll; the next, rocking and rolling with his guitar opening a show for his hero, Elvis Presley. It's a pretty sure bet that he preferred the second of the two engagements!

There's not too much to add about Elvis at this particular juncture except to emphasise again how incredibly busy he was and how exhausting a schedule he was continuing to operate. Believe it or not, after that early evening showroom opening and the performance at Fair Park, he also played a late-night show at the Cotton Club: three appearances within the space of just twenty-four hours!

It was here that Buddy's school pal, Jerry Allison, witnessed the Great White Wonder for the first time. Though only sixteen, Jerry had already been playing drums for some time with a local hillbilly outfit called Cal Wayne & The Riverside Ranch Hands and, as with Buddy, his imagination was set alight by the pulsating new music of Elvis Presley: 'The first time I saw Elvis, I was amazed. I went and bought both records he had out. Elvis, Jim Ed Brown and some other performers had done a performance at the Fair Park Coliseum. I was with Cal Wayne and we were playing the Cotton Club. We played a dance and then after the show, Elvis and a few performers from the Fair Park would come out and do a short show and get $25 apiece to appear at the Cotton Club. Elvis was backstage carrying in amps, and I thought: look at how that fellow's dressed — very strange! He had on something like an orange shirt, yellow coat and purple pants or something. I packed my stuff away and sat in the audience. When Elvis started to play and I couldn't believe it. It was *so* 'rock & roll'. It was something I'd never seen.'

Future Cricket Joe B. Mauldin (at that time bass-player with the Four Teens) was similarly impressed: 'I was already into Elvis' records. He was on Sun at the time, and every time a new record came out I bought it and everybody in our group learned it. When I saw Elvis at the Fair Park, I flipped! I was ready to start being a musician and making a living at it. I went to the Cotton Club after the Coliseum show and got to sit in the car and visit with Elvis a little bit. To me he was the greatest thing I ever saw.'

As if his intensive itinerary of tour dates were not enough, Presley also managed to squeeze in a broadcast from the *Big D Jamboree* in Dallas two weeks later, as well as several *Louisiana Hayride* appearances during that month. His jaunts throughout Texas at this time must have seemed neverending, but things would soon change and not even the hectic years immediately ahead would come close to rivalling his punishing 1955 schedule.

From what's been documented thus far, it's a stone certainty that Presley and Holly knew one another, but given the maelstrom that was the former's life it's equally probable that they never really had the opportunity to develop more than a superficial relationship. Elvis must literally have met hundreds of fans, musicians, deejays and reporters throughout the whole of that crazy year as he continued to barnstorm the South.

It's about here in our story that things get rather complicated — particularly for Jerry Allison. Coming from a country music tradition, Buddy was in two minds as to whether to add drums to his group, or to make do with the rhythm that the slap bass could provide. Whenever he appeared in Lubbock, Elvis was backed only by Scotty and Bill, but Buddy had also seen him on a televised *Louisiana Hayride* show that March with house drummer D.J. Fontana in support (albeit tactfully concealed behind a curtain). To confuse matters further, the top deck of his recent hit single, *Baby Let's Play House* belted along with just the drummer-less trio for accompaniment, while the equally-popular flip, *I'm Left, You're Right, She's Gone*, definitely *did* have someone beating the skins on it!

Jerry did quite a bit of hanging around while his friend made up his mind which way to jump, but by the year end no question mark existed and he became a permanent fixture essential to Buddy's developing sound.

5th visit: Saturday, 15 October 1955 at the Fair Park Coliseum and the Cotton Club

When Elvis returned four and a half months later for his final visit that year, his fifth single, *Mystery Train* b/w *I Forgot To Remember To Forget* was doing brisk business* and he was hotter than a firecracker. He'd even briefly become too hot for his own Cadillac, which burst into flames shortly after an appearance in his old home town of Tupelo!

He was now busier than ever, with no let-up in his touring schedule. And, as if life wasn't hectic enough, there were also other tensions to contend with as the jockeying continued over who would end up as his long-term manager. Bob Neal still officially had the job, but was becoming increasingly sidelined as Colonel Tom Parker now handled almost 100% of his bookings through his Jamboree Attractions. These bookings were becoming more and more lucrative as the gate monies continued to escalate, and Neal had little option but to take a back seat, even if for now Presley's parents — particularly Gladys — preferred him to the scheming carny. The end of Bob Neal's short reign was indeed nigh, a sacrifice that sadly seemed inevitable if Elvis was ever to maximise his obvious potential.

Sam Phillips at Sun was also about to become another sacrificial victim, compelled by financial circumstances to sell Elvis' contract to RCA,

---

* It turned out to be his most successful release to date, eventually becoming his first country chart-topper.

So 'rock & roll': Elvis backstage at the Overton Park Shell, Memphis on 5 August 1955.

although he at least ended up with a respectable cash settlement to offset his pain. This gave him the opportunity to plough more monies into developing other artists like Carl Perkins, Johnny Cash and Jerry Lee Lewis who were showing a definite potential of their own in the slipstream created by Presley.

Someone who had already made that elusive breakthrough and had

Bill and Elvis pictured in Cleveland, Ohio on 19 October 1955.

reached No. 1 in the *Billboard* 'Top 100' with *Rock Around The Clock* was Bill Haley from Philadelphia. With particularly fortuitous timing, the Colonel did a deal with Haley's manager, Lord Jim Ferguson, for Elvis to tour together with him and Hank Snow from early October 1955 onwards.

In fact, Haley and his Comets were booked to play Lubbock on Friday, 14 October, while Elvis headlined another show there the following night. At other venues they shared the same bill which — come to think of it — must have been great value for money! Interestingly, there was a common factor linking those consecutive appearances of Haley and Presley at Lubbock, and the reader can by now probably guess who or what this was. Yes, once again that well-known local turn, Lubbock's own Buddy & Bob, was slated to open both shows.

Haley had been a constant presence in the *Billboard* 'Top 100' for most of the year with *Rock Around The Clock* and several smaller hits, and was now a major attraction throughout the country. Hell, he could even impress those Texans! Seriously though, the fact was that he could carry a show and draw a crowd at venues such as Lubbock without a need for the usual big package, and so that night only Buddy & Bob and Jimmie Rodgers Snow were booked as support. Besides, the promoters probably wouldn't have been able to pay many more artists after meeting Haley's asking price!

Buddy & Bob of course were still at least a couple of steps behind everyone else, although they had made some minor progress over the past couple of months. Briefly, the annual *South Plains Fair* had come around again to the Lubbock area that September, and the duo (this time accompanied by Don Guess on bass and Sonny Curtis on fiddle and guitar) got to play a whole bunch of small nearby rural venues over a three-day period as part of a big promotional shebang. Alas, they didn't get to travel in

THE
RHYTHM AND BLUES
SONGSTERS OF
"SHAKE, RATTLE, AND
ROLL" FAME

BILL HALEY
AND HIS COMETS

FRIDAY
OCTOBER 14th
8:00 P.M.
FAIR PARK
COLISEUM

EIGHT STRAIGHT
RECORDING HITS
INCLUDING

"Shake, Rattle and Roll"
"Rock Around the Clock"
"Dim, Dim The Lights"

PLUS
JIMMY RODGERS SNOW

RCA VICTOR ARTIST
AND
SON OF THE FAMOUS HANK SNOW

PLUS
LUBBOCK'S OWN
BUDDY, BOB AND LARRY

DON'T MISS THIS
BIG
ROCK AND ROLL SHOW

a Cadillac like Elvis, but were simply bussed around the Texas countryside — which probably didn't do a great deal for their egos.

They'd also cut several professional demos that summer at the Nesman studios in Wichita Falls in the hope of securing that all-important record deal. They even had a clutch of demo records to hand out if only someone — anyone — would just give them a listen.

A potentially lucky break occurred that night when Haley arrived in town to find that his Comets and their musical gear hadn't yet shown up, having been stranded somewhere on the way in a broken-down vehicle. It seemed for a while that the headliner wouldn't be able to appear at all until the promoters suggested to Bill that there were couple of local lads[*] who could back him up until the Comets arrived, if he was willing to give it a shot. Thus it was that Haley and Holly got to meet for the very first time on stage that night when the rookie Comets played backup for around thirty minutes until the regular band finally arrived and Mafeking was relieved. Perhaps this and other such moments can all be collected under that ubiquitous phrase 'paying your dues'. Either way, it was an experience that Buddy would certainly not have forgotten in a hurry.

The following night, it was back to the usual formula as Elvis — still not always a sole headliner — appeared alongside a cluster of country acts including Jimmy 'C' Newman, Bobby Lord, Jimmy Day, Floyd Cramer (shortly to begin a long association with Elvis as session pianist at RCA) and openers Buddy & Bob. Additionally, for

---

[*] Holly historian John Ingman has a 1963 interview with Mrs. Holley in which she states that Bob Montgomery was not with Buddy on this show, and it was more likely Sonny Curtis on guitar and Larry Welborn on bass. However, Curtis recently confirmed that he was not present.

Already a dynamic performer: Buddy on stage at Lubbock Legion Hall on 15 April 1955 with Sonny Curtis (lead guitar), Jerry Allison (drums) and [not visible] Don Guess (bass).

the first time ever in Lubbock, there was an unfamiliar name added for the locals to run their eyes over — a new protégé of Sam Phillips by the name of Johnny Cash.

What a good ol' Southern night that must have been, with Cash belting out *Cry! Cry! Cry!* and *Hey! Porter* from his recent debut single (which, in a clear parallel to Presley, was creating a considerable stir in Southern regional markets but not much beyond).

Frustrating as it was for Phillips, he just couldn't get his records distributed further afield no matter how hard he tried. Back in 1955 the infrastructure just wasn't there — despite the fact that Sun now had some forty distributors — although the majors would not remain in the driving seat much longer. Even so, financial pressures compelled him several weeks later to sell his biggest asset — Elvis Presley — to the highest bidder. On Monday, 21 November 1955, Sam's golden boy signed the contract with RCA-Victor that would usher in a new era in popular music and bring him undreamt-of wealth and fame.

Remarkably, within a couple of weeks of Elvis making the big time, Buddy also achieved a significant career breakthrough. On 28 October, while appearing on a country bill with Autry Inman, Hank Locklin, Mitchell Torok, Porter Wagoner and Slim Whitman, he was befriended by headliner Marty Robbins, who spent some time with him dispensing advice.

It was probably at Marty's instigation that his Nashville agent, Eddie

Fair Park Coliseum, 10 April 1955: Elvis (far right) waves to an approaching Sonny Curtis (white shirt, centre of picture). On the far left, Don Guess looks in Elvis' direction, while next to him a strangely disinterested Buddy and Jerry Allison watch the band performing on stage.

Crandall, cabled Dave Stone at KDAV two weeks later asking him to get Buddy to cut some demos on acetate and mail them to talent scout Jim Denny up in Nashville. This he did in early December. After initially drawing a blank at Columbia, Denny tried Decca's local A&R man, Paul Cohen, and the rest — as they say — is history.

6th visit: Tuesday, 10 April 1956 at the Fair Park Coliseum

When Elvis returned to Lubbock the following April for what was to be his last visit to the city until November 1972, *Heartbreak Hotel* — his first national pop hit — was a couple of weeks off hitting the top of the *Billboard* 'Top 100' and he was finally on the road to stardom. He was reported to have been paid $4,000 for the show, which also featured Faron Young, Wanda Jackson and Jimmy & Johnny. Local photographer Isaac Holmes took some backstage shots of him after the event, in which Bob Montgomery and Larry Welborn also appear. Buddy, however, is conspicuous by his absence.

Needless to say, he *was* there — it would have been inconceivable for him not to turn out to see his hero — and can plainly be identified on the grainy snapshot included here, taken by a Presley fan from Austin. Also in the picture are Don Guess and Sonny Curtis (with whom Buddy toured on

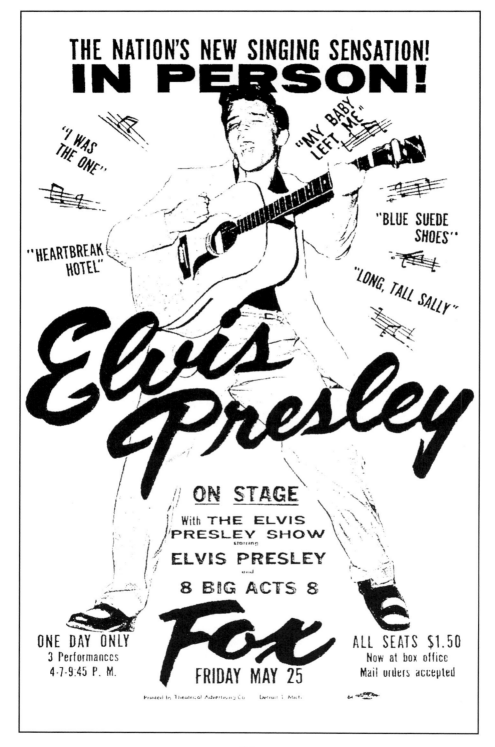

Still from the historic Ben Hall film. Buddy is flanked by Hall (left) and Sonny Curtis.

and off during April and May that year supporting Sonny James) and Jerry Allison. Unfortunately, it is not known whether the boys backed James when he played Lubbock on 26 April.

Then there is the mystery of the now-legendary home movie shot by local radio personality/bandleader Ben Hall. This fascinating length of celluloid includes what is reputed to be the earliest footage of Elvis Presley in action, as well as various scenes of Holly, Presley, Johnny Cash and Carl Perkins backstage.

Hall claims to have shot the film at a concert in Lubbock in 1955, but there was never a single occasion — either in 1955 or since — when all the personalities featured appeared on the same bill. Moreover, Presley's attire is more redolent of his 1956 stage garb than the styles he wore in 1955, and Perkins' quite obvious references to his 'blue suede shoes' likewise firmly place the event post-1955.

The most likely explanation is that the Elvis footage dates from his 10 April 1956 appearance in Lubbock, and that Hall finished off his film at another Fair Park show on 26 April 1956 which included Perkins, Johnny Cash, Sonny James, Justin Tubb and the Belew Twins.

We know that Buddy and his group were present on the first of these occasions and may also have been around on the second, either as spectators or playing backup for Sonny James. However, the latter is uncertain as no record exists of them being on the bill on that date. Then

---

* Extracts from the film were featured in the 1985 BBC2 *Arena* TV documentary, *Buddy Holly* (later extended and repackaged on video by MPL as *The Real Buddy Holly Story*).

again, backing bands and minor support acts were often not advertised.

Also seen bobbing about in the background during the Elvis segment of the film is a dark-haired lass in a red cowgirl outfit, who looks very much like *Big D Jamboree* regular Helen Hall (no relation to Ben). As with Buddy, there is no evidence of her being on the bill that night.

There are so many stories of Buddy and his friends running around with Elvis in Lubbock that they are too numerous either to list or discount. Some concern a visit to the local cinema, others drinking Cokes in a cafe, or cruising down to a local hot-spot called the Hi-D-Ho Drive In. Whatever the meetings may have been, they almost certainly didn't include a historical tour of the city! Ultimately, however, whilst one or two recollections of such happenings may have been embroidered or appear somewhat fanciful, it is clear that Elvis and Buddy did form a brief friendship during those few hectic, energy-filled months.

There is, however, one particular anecdote which it would be criminal to omit. It relates to Buddy's steady girlfriend from school, Echo McGuire, with whom he was to split up in late 1955. She recalls with some amusement that Buddy took her to see his hero at the Cotton Club and, upon being introduced to him, was asked for a kiss — which she demurely declined! She thereby claims to be the first female to deny Elvis such a request... and that might just be the truth!

Musical Interlude #6

Are You Lonesome To-night? **recorded by Elvis Presley on 4 April 1960 at RCA Studio B, Nashville, Tennessee.**
*Peggy Sue***, recorded by Buddy Holly late June/early July 1957 at the Norman Petty Recording Studio in Clovis, New Mexico.**

On the face of it, there is little to connect the above recordings with one another except that both were massive hits in the USA and the United Kingdom. But they do raise the intriguing subject of 'answer' records that were in vogue during the Fifties and early Sixties, so it's interesting to look at them in some detail.

In the wake of the No. 1 success of *It's Now Or Never* (based on the Italian aria, *O Sole Mio*, written in 1901 and famously recorded by Enrico Caruso in 1916), Elvis — reportedly at the instigation of his manager — decided to revive another old song called *Are You Lonesome To-night?* Written by Roy Turk and Lon Handman, two Tin Pan Alley songsmiths, it had first been recorded in 1926 by Al Jolson and soon after by a lady called Vaughn Deleath, for whom it became a hit in 1927.

Presley's version (a direct copy of Jolson's) provided him with yet another Transatlantic chart-topper and not unexpectedly inspired a flurry of 'answer' records, three of which made the lower rungs of the US charts the same year. Needless to say, all were from ladies — very possibly as a direct response to the smouldering spoken interlude.

Highest-placed (at No. 55 in the *Billboard* 'Hot 100') was the Thelma Carpenter effort entitled *Yes, I'm Lonesome Tonight*, while the same title by

---

*   It is interesting to note that the narrative (which was based on Jacques' speech from Shakespeare's *As You Like It*) was also part of the original composition, not an Elvis add-on.

Dodie Stevens made No. 60. Another 'answer', Jeanne Black's *Oh, How I Miss You Tonight*, climbed to a lowly No. 63. Ms. Black had, in fact, inaugurated her career as a hitmaker several months before with *He'll Have To Stay*, a response to Jim Reeves' *He'll Have To Go*.

One year earlier, meanwhile, Buddy Holly had bucked the trend and — most unusually — recorded an 'answer' to one of his own records, *Peggy Sue*.

The idea for *Peggy Sue Got Married* was apparently suggested to him by his father and, desperate for another hit at this stage of his career, the singer worked on the lyrics and committed them to tape at his New York apartment. Overdubbed by Coral in their New York studios later that year, it became the first posthumous Holly release to dent the UK Top Twenty.

Although he may have felt that it had hit potential, Buddy could never have envisaged that his song title would one day inspire both a movie and a stage show of the same name decades after he left that initial run-through on his Ampex tape recorder.

Elvis, of course, had neither the need nor the desire to record 'answers' to anybody's records, least of all his own.

---

* Fans with long memories will recall that *It Doesn't Matter Anymore* was released shortly before his death.

- CHAPTER 7 -

A Shooting Star Falls To Earth

Rave on

So what became of Buddy Holly after that first eventful year of 1955, when he crossed paths several times with the charmed Elvis Presley? In recent years, his life has been documented and analysed in some depth, even if those investigations pale in comparison with the dissection that has been carried out on Elvis. The written word apropos Holly can never begin to compare with the avalanche of books on Presley — many with such unlikely titles as *The Day Elvis Met Nixon, Elvis Files – Was His Death Faked?* or *Over The Fence: A Neighbor's Memories Of Elvis.* The reader can also surf the net and readily discover and visit any number of weird Elvis websites. It truly seems that curiosity as to his life knows no bounds. But let us stick with the factual stuff while occasionally drawing attention to oft-overlooked or minor snippets of information where they may be of interest. Perhaps we can also correct some of the usual shibboleths in the process.

What are we hinting at here? Well, trivial it may be, but for example Buddy Holly is usually described as some kind of gangling giant, while in reality he was of no more than average height (5 feet 11 inches, for the record). And, while he may have seemed like Mister Nice Guy to his fans, Sonny Curtis remembers that he was often a smart alec, loud and headstrong. Similarly, Norman Petty's recollections were that 'No-one could ever tell Buddy Holly what to do. Not you, not me, not anyone.' So, it seems that, like many of us, he could be a different person to different people.

More recently, the *Buddy* musical has continued to portray Ritchie Valens as a hip-swivelling Chicano version of Presley, which likewise bears little relation to the truth. The Big Bopper is consistently quoted as having been born in 1932 (1930 is in fact the correct year) — a simple error that has been repeated so often that it now seems impossible to correct. As for Elvis, legend has him starting out as a denim-clad truck driver, whilst his first job was actually as a lowly-paid apprentice at Parker Machines.

The literature regarding many of the artists from the Fifties is littered with such irritating inaccuracies and the hope is that not too many are perpetuated here. Without becoming too serious about the subject, it is suggested that discerning readers seek out specialist music writers and avoid those that recycle old clichés by failing to check the simplest of facts. Of course, anyone working in the legal profession would readily confirm that proving the most basic of facts is often far from easy, and the passage of time makes it even harder to nail down that elusive and shifting truth. Sadly, it seems that once something has been said in print and repeated a few times, it becomes carved in stone and like the proverbial supertanker becomes almost impossible to turn around. Let's see if we can set the record straight.

If you see old Annie better give her a lift

We take up the story at the beginning of 1956 with Buddy having finally been offered a record deal thanks largely to the efforts of Marty Robbins' agent, Eddie Crandall. Inevitably, his acceptance of a solo recording contract resulted in the break-up of the Buddy, Bob and Larry aggregation, although the parting itself was amicable. Bob Montgomery was happy to return to his favoured country music, while bassist Larry Welborn (who was still at school) switched to lead guitar and joined the Four Teens.

By mid-January the name of Buddy Holly* had been added to Decca's small roster of rockabilly acts in a relationship that must have looked full of promise to the young Texan. In fact, he would achieve only limited success until he came back to the same label the following year as the leader of a quartet called the Crickets.

It all started off pretty positively though, with a debut recording session quickly lined up at the famous Bradley's Barn studio in Nashville for 26 January. Arriving in the future country capital with Sonny Curtis and Don Guess in tow, it really must have seemed to Buddy just for a brief moment that he'd finally made it and that that fabled Cadillac would soon be coming his way. But it was not to be. Producer Owen Bradley and his session musicians were steeped in country music tradition and didn't really understand how to record rock & roll; for their part, Holly and his friends had no idea about how go about making a commercial recording. Two further sessions in July and November proved similarly disappointing, with largely unsympathetic productions that never really took off.

During the course of those three sessions in January, July and November 1956, eleven different titles** were committed to tape. None of these is especially well known, although they did include Buddy's first attempt at *That'll Be The Day*, which he and Jerry Allison had written together shortly after hearing John Wayne repeatedly utter those immortal words in one of the all-time great westerns, *The Searchers*.

On this occasion, the number was sung in a disconcertingly high register by Holly and is markedly different to the following year's hit recording with the Crickets — though nowhere near different enough to justify producer Norman Petty claiming a composer credit!

---

* The oft-related story is that the person responsible for typing Buddy's contract accidentally omitted the 'e' from his surname and that, rather than complain, he simply decided to run with 'Holly'. It seems far more probable, however, that he made a conscious decision to adopt the name at this time after seeing it frequently mis-spelt throughout his life. It is also likely that the neatness and symmetry of 'Buddy Holly' would have appealed to his artistic sensibilities. Either way, it is an intriguing coincidence that, while Buddy lost the 'e' from his surname via his Decca contract, Elvis Presley lost an 'a' from his middle name when it was incorrectly spelt 'Aron' on his birth certificate — an error he later had corrected.

** The rockabilly-styled Sonny Curtis composition *Rock Around With Ollie Vee* — probably the strongest number — was attempted at two of the Nashville sessions but was not released as a single until the following year when Holly finally became hot property.

Sonny Curtis, Buddy Holly and Don Guess on tour in Odessa, Texas in May 1956.

Most intriguing of all the tracks is one from the first Nashville session in January 1956 — not penned by Buddy, but similar in style to the notorious *'Annie'* recordings of the Midnighters such as *Work With Me Annie* and *Annie Had A Baby*. Although they didn't cross over into the pop mainstream, both records had topped the *Billboard* R&B chart in 1954 and represented just one tiny part of the ingredients that went to make up the rich panoply of early rock & roll.

In fact, *Midnight Shift* jumped squarely onto that whole *'Annie'* bandwagon, although it had actually been written under an alias by country songwriter Luke McDaniel and had no connection whatsoever with Hank Ballard. It also contained quite risqué lyrics for that era — especially for a white artist — dealing as it did with so-called 'ladies of the night'. This probably explains why it wasn't included on either of the Holly singles put out that year by Decca — at that time a decidedly conservative organisation — although it eventually appeared as a single in the UK several years later.

---

* The song is well known to British fans as it was rush-released in the aftermath of the 1959 crash and got to No.26 in the *NME* 'Top 30'. These days, it is also acclaimed as an prime example of early rockabilly — that vibrant but hard-to-define sub-genre of rock & roll.

*Holding Bob Montgomery's Gibson guitar, nineteen year old
Buddy poses for a Decca publicity shot, January 1956.*

Of the remaining songs, *Ting-A-Ling* (a 1952 hit for the Clovers) is the only one that had any real history, but neither it nor *That'll Be The Day* was deemed worthy of release at the time. Instead, *Blue Days, Black Nights* (a Ben Hall composition) was selected for his debut single in April 1956, followed by *Modern Don Juan* (written by Don Guess and Jack Neal) in December. The records were given little publicity outside of the usual trade reviews and hardly surprisingly sank without trace.

The contrast between Holly and Elvis Presley could not have been more marked at this juncture. While Buddy was struggling to get off the ground, the Elvis juggernaut had been tearing the country apart, racking up an amazing seventeen *Billboard* 'Top 100' hits during the course of that year including five Number Ones (*Heartbreak Hotel, I Want You, I Need You, I Love You, Don't Be Cruel, Hound Dog* and *Love Me Tender*). Clearly, he still had a long way to go to catch up with his idol.

Down the line to Clovis

There's a contemporary quote that Buddy was 'pretty darn discouraged' when the option on his Decca deal wasn't renewed at the beginning of 1957, but within weeks he was back in the studio cutting demos — if anything, more determined than ever to succeed in the business. If Elvis had hit the big time, then why couldn't he? Buddy was, it seems, the most stubborn of individuals once he'd set his mind on something, so there was never a single moment when he'd considered quitting. It was also around now that independent producer Norman Petty began to figure prominently in his story — despite the fact that he's conspicuously absent in the only film made of the singer's life.

Petty is a particularly interesting character and — in the author's opinion — was not the weirdo portrayed by some writers on the life and times of Buddy Holly. Of course, like all human beings he had his faults, but he was certainly no Svengali figure. A fair summary of his relationship with Holly might perhaps be best expressed as: 'Norman needed Buddy, and Buddy needed Norman'.

Petty, himself a relatively young man not quite than ten years older than Holly, had started out in the radio business as a radio announcer in Clovis, but it was an radio engineer that he really shone and was to initially make his mark. After an enforced stint in the USAF, he returned to Clovis in 1955 and with the help of his new wife Vi opened a recording studio which quickly gained a reputation for its state-of-the-art equipment.

He'd also formed his own group — the Norman Petty Trio — back in 1949, since when they had became quite a popular outfit (their 1954 hit, *Mood Indigo*, helped to finance the building of the studio). In fact, things were going so well for the trio at this point, that it really must have been quite a wrench to have to mothball his own musical ambitions a few months later when the Crickets suddenly broke nationally with *That'll Be The Day* creating a demand for more of the same.[*] It is plain even from those few facts that Petty was as far removed from being a Colonel Parker as it is possible to imagine.

Returning to the subject of the *Buddy Holly Story* biopic, it really seems incredible that such a film could be made without any mention of Norman Petty, producer, mentor and eventual manager of Buddy Holly up until the latter days of his career. Petty was reportedly approached to become involved but declined. Mind you, Holly's unique voice was not used for the film either. Rather, it was decided to use Gary Busey's vocals cut live in an attempt to create an exciting atmosphere.[**] Despite these negatives (and a dedicated Holly fan could certainly list quite a few others!), the film was well received and is fondly remembered.

Holly, who died aged twenty-two, is played with intensity by the

[*] The Norman Petty Trio's recording of *Almost Paradise* entered the *Billboard* 'Top 100' chart on 23 February 1957 — the same weekend that Holly and the Crickets were busy cutting *That'll Be The Day*. Both were of course produced at Petty's Clovis studio.

[**] Although an actor, Busey had been a working musician for some time fronting minor bands like Teddy Jack Eddy and Carp, so perhaps it wasn't the huge risk it might have seemed to let him loose on the Buddy Holly songbook.

*Norman Petty (left) and Buddy Holly receive a gold disc from
Coral/Brunswick's Bob Thiele for sales of 'Peggy Sue'.*

thirty-three year old Busey, who deservedly received a 'Best Actor' nomination for his portrayal of the singer, even if those who remember Buddy could not wholly relate to his musical performances. 'Gary Busey plays Chuck Berry' was the assessment of one who knew him well, the ever-honest Sonny Curtis.

Other inaccuracies include giving Lubbock a mountainous landscape — in fact the area is quite flat, as the word 'plains' implies — and the scene straight out of a scriptwriter's fantasy world where an angry Holly knocks down his first Nashville producer, the highly respected Owen Bradley! Again, Sonny Curtis, who played on some of those Nashville recordings, states far more accurately and with some feeling that the Lubbock youngsters' attitude to their producer back then was: 'Yes sir, no sir, certainly Mr. Bradley, sir!' Rebellion, it seems, was definitely not part of their agenda.

Despite its shortcomings, the big 'plus' of the film was that it brought Buddy Holly's name back on the scene in his homeland, where it had largely been forgotten until Don McLean's 1971 hit, *American Pie*, sparked a renewal of interest in the singer. The *Buddy Holly Story* film, released a few years later in 1978, effectively completed his rehabilitation. (As an aside, isn't it particularly ironic that the Holly movie went into production late in 1977 — literally within weeks of Elvis' sudden passing?)

Back now to Buddy's career, and it's interesting to note that, in between his first and second visits to Nashville, he also made his first visit to Norman Petty's studio in Clovis*, where he cut several demos that were far more upbeat than any he had done back in Texas. Later in the year, he laid down some equally uptempo rehearsal tracks at the tiny Venture Studio in Lubbock. Ironically, these included several numbers from Elvis' repertoire including *Good Rockin' Tonight*, *Rip It Up*, *Blue Suede Shoes* and *Shake, Rattle & Roll*. Who knows, Holly may have had more hit potential had he recorded such covers (look at Pat Boone!), but Decca were only tentatively beginning to dip their toes into the rock & roll whirlpool and — as the saying goes — he was simply in the wrong place at the right time.**

The Crickets finally get to chirp

Fame finally put in an appearance in 1957 when Buddy re-cut *That'll Be The Day* at Norman Petty's studio in late February with Jerry Allison on drums, Larry Welborn on bass*** and new face Niki Sullivan replacing Sonny Curtis on rhythm guitar. *I'm Looking For Someone To Love*, hastily written the night before, was recorded for the flip. This time, however, Holly was in control, and the cuts turned out sounding ten times better than Decca's 'professionally-recorded' efforts of the previous year. All were convinced of the coupling's hit potential, but before that could happen there were a couple of matters that required some attention.

First and foremost, there was the troublesome standard clause in Buddy's Decca contract which prohibited him from re-recording any material for any other label for a period of five years — a condition he was unable to extricate himself from, despite a lengthy telephone call to Paul Cohen. The obvious solution was a name change, and out of this necessity the Crickets were born.

Secondly, there was the minor matter of getting a record company interested. Of course, Norman Petty could simply have released the record on one of his own small labels, but he knew he had to sign the group to a major if he was to achieve any real success for Buddy and the boys. Fortunately, through his activities as a successful musician, composer and producer, he was relatively well-connected in the music business and he pushed the demo tape to Murray Deutsch at Peer-Southern Music, a company he had ties with. Deutsch liked what he heard, but struggled to

---

* The quiet town of Clovis lies a little over one hundred miles due west of Lubbock, just inside the New Mexico border. Originally built at a junction on the Santa Fe Railroad known as Riley's Switch, it was renamed 'Clovis' (after the Fifth Century Frankish king) at the suggestion of a railroad official's daughter who came across it in a history book.

** Whilst it may appear contradictory that Gene Vincent had recorded the frantic *Be-Bop-A-Lula* at that same Nashville studio for Capitol in May 1956, he worked with a different producer to the one that Decca had assigned to Holly.

*** Shortly after the session, Welborn was replaced in the group by the Four Teens' bassist, Joe B. Mauldin.

Jerry, Buddy and Joe B. rehearse 'That'll Be The Day' at the home of June Clark, a friend of the group, circa February 1957.

place the product. Atlantic, Columbia and RCA all turned him down flat.

Finally, he managed to get Coral's A&R director, Bob Thiele, interested but, due to concerns about image and commerciality, Thiele was unable to persuade his senior management to sign the Crickets. Thiele persisted however, and was eventually given approval to put their record out on a subsidiary label, Brunswick. Against expectations he immediately released the demo he'd been sent by Petty — a superb production which he rightly felt could hardly be bettered.

The Crickets' first release hit the racks in May 1957, but it didn't enter the national charts until August after it had been played non-stop by Guy King of WWOL in Buffalo, New York, who effectively 'broke' the record (though not quite as dramatically as the *Buddy Holly Story* film would have us believe). In the end, Thiele's faith proved to be well placed: *That'll Be The Day* hit the No. 1 spot in September and was also certified as a million-seller that same month.

On reflection, that half year wait between cutting the demo and the record becoming a hit must have seemed interminable to Buddy and his friends. Yet, they seemed to have an unflinching faith in their destiny, and incredibly already had classics such as *Oh Boy!* and *Peggy Sue* in the can even before their first release had charted! That fact continues to amaze even now. As with the Beatles several years later, the amount of quality material recorded was staggering, with 'B' sides (what a dated expression

that now seems!) often equalling if not surpassing the 'A' sides. If we remind ourselves that *Everyday* by Holly and the perennial *Eleanor Rigby* by the Beatles were both 'B' sides, that should help make the point.

Perhaps the biggest irony of all was that, by signing to Brunswick, the Crickets effectively became Decca recording artists — the same parent company who had put out Buddy's first two unsuccessful Nashville singles and to whom he was still contracted as a solo act!

Life for the next twelve months was a rollercoaster ride for the group, with a string of hits[*] including *Oh Boy!*, *Peggy Sue*, *Maybe Baby*, *Rave On*, *Think It Over* and *Early In The Morning*, and non-stop tours sandwiching national TV appearances without a break. Their success quickly spread overseas too, leading to tours in 1958 of both Britain and Australia that are fondly remembered to the present day.

Before 1957 was out, however, the pressure of touring got to rhythm guitarist Niki Sullivan and he left the group. He'd played on almost all the tracks that made up the classic *Chirping Crickets* album — one of only two long-players released during Holly's lifetime — and therefore certainly deserves to be more than just a footnote in his story. Although no longer part of the music business except for special occasions, he remains justly proud of the small but important contribution he made to the group's original sound, both at Clovis and during their first major tours.

Following Sullivan's departure to briefly attempt a solo career, the Crickets became a three-piece and remained so for most of 1958, when yet another important development came about. This brought talented lead guitarist Tommy Allsup (who, like Holly, also favoured the Fender Strat) into the picture, after he had initially been hired to play lead on several studio tracks including *Heartbeat* and *Love's Made A Fool Of You*. He would later join Buddy for the final two tours of his career and, of course, the tale has been told over and over as to how Ritchie Valens stole Tommy's plane seat from under his nose by winning it with the fateful toss of a coin. As far as it's possible to ascertain, the story of the flipped coin seems to be true and Allsup went on in later years to run a club with the dubious title of Tommy's Heads-Up!

True love ways

1958 was to be a watershed year for Buddy in other ways too, resulting from his marriage to Maria Elena Santiago, a secretary with his New York publishers, Peer-Southern whom he'd first met earlier that year when visiting their offices. Although the couple had known each another for some time, the decision to wed was evidently taken unexpectedly following Buddy's return from headlining the *Summer Dance Party* tour in July. The ceremony took place at his parents' home on 15 August and was conducted by his pastor, Ben Johnson, who sadly was to officiate at a much less joyous ritual for Buddy only six months later.

Within weeks, he decided to relocate to New York to be with his wife, opting for life in an apartment near Greenwich Village rather than a home on the range. The move precipitated a split with his friends and long-time backing musicians Jerry Allison and Joe B. Mauldin, and subsequently with his manager Norman Petty, who the ambitious Buddy increasingly felt was

---

[*] Such was the group's intense creativity at this point, that Bob Thiele — in cahoots with Norman Petty — decided to double up, issuing material with backing vocals by the Picks (or later the Roses) under the Crickets' name on Brunswick — the label Decca normally used for their 'race' recordings — while solo releases by Buddy Holly without backing vocals simultaneously appeared on Coral. To add to the confusion, Decca also attempted to grab a piece of the action for themselves with three further releases of Buddy's Nashville material during the course of 1957-58, including the original (inferior) version of *That'll Be The Day*.

The Crickets at work in the Clovis studio, December 1957, cutting 'Little Baby'.
On the far left is session pianist and co-composer C.W.Kendall Jr.

being small-minded and holding back his career in a variety of ways. What was markedly different between these new developments was that whilst the parting with his group was completely without rancour — albeit intensely sad for all concerned — that with Petty was to become increasingly acrimonious, and perhaps even indirectly led to the singer's untimely death.

Put simply, by Christmas 1958 Buddy had little alternative but to sign up with the GAC Agency to go on that final *Winter Dance Party* tour in the frozen Midwest. He may have had misgivings, but he needed to ease the cash-flow problems that the split with the Crickets had precipitated.

To briefly act as Devil's advocate, it was inevitable that monies owed to the group would have to be frozen for a while to work out how they would subsequently need to be shared, particularly as no songwriting agreements had ever been drawn up in those heady early days. However, the forever-impetuous Holly was certainly not going to hang around waiting for months while matters were sorted out, so he simply engaged a New York lawyer and carried on recording and touring.

One particular gripe that Holly had with Petty was his apathy in getting him an appearance in any of the rash of rock & roll movies that had flooded the market during the late Fifties. Although many were quick cash-ins, the publicity was invaluable and Jerry Lee Lewis, Carl Perkins, Buddy's Texan pals Buddy Knox and Jimmy Bowen and virtually all the other main protagonists made at

---

He reportedly also tried to persuade his friend Eddie Cochran to join the tour — unsuccessfully as it happens — but even so, the latter's date with destiny was not to be long delayed when the road ran out for him just fifteen months later. Incredible as it seems, at the time of Cochran's fatal accident on 17 April 1960, Buddy's former chums, Jerry Allison, Sonny Curtis and Joe B. Mauldin were touring England with the Everly Brothers and were close to the hospital where Eddie was taken. Isn't Greek tragedy mixed up in all of this somewhere?

The Crickets share some bonhomie with members of the Big Beats outside the Clovis studio. Left to right: Jerry Zapata, Donny McCord, Jerry Allison, Earl Slocomb, Buddy Holly and Joe B. Mauldin.

least one silver screen appearance and some several. Buddy was one of a handful that never got the chance — almost certainly due to the attitude of the ultra-conservative Petty — although the Crickets did eventually appear in *Just For Fun* in the early Sixties following his death. Only Elvis Presley could really afford to opt out of such film offers, secure in the knowledge that he had got a contract to star in his very own movies.

One wonders, perhaps unkindly, whether Petty feared his own influence would wane if Holly were to spread his wings and move into this different medium? It's certainly a possibility. The opinion of Jerry Zapata, a member of the Big Beats who were for a time the house band at Clovis, is that, although Petty was a great engineer and producer, he was definitely 'all for Norman'. Although it's largely academic now, it is nevertheless intriguing to shed light on these aspects of Holly's career even at this late date.

One last thought for now on Norman Petty. Since his death from leukaemia back in 1984, it has been open season to attack him and the scales are now probably tipped too far in the wrong direction. Although he clearly had faults, there is absolutely no doubt that Buddy Holly needed Norman Petty at the start and this fact cannot just be airbrushed out. It is by no means certain that he would have ever got that first major break without Petty, his studio and the whole unique set-up that he had created in the middle of Nowheresville, New Mexico — coincidentally located conveniently near to where Buddy happened to live. Petty also went on to have hits with several other acts including the Fireballs and the String-A-Longs, even though he's rightly best remembered for his classic productions with Holly and the Crickets.

In the final analysis, Holly's marriage turned out to be more of a turning point than he might have expected. Although *Early In The Morning* got to No. 32 in the *Billboard* 'Hot 100' that summer (the flip, *Now We're One*, was played at his wedding), he was to score only one minor hit during the remaining six months of his life. But, if his career was stuttering at the end of 1958, is it really possible that his successes were all in the past? Surely not. What is a fact though, is that at the time of his death, the seventeen year old Ritchie Valens was the one at the top of the US charts, and some news reports of the tragedy led with his death as the headline with the names of Holly and the Big Bopper coming below.[*]

There's not a cloud to spoil the view

An entire book (*The Day The Music Died* by Larry Lehmer) has been written about the *Winter Dance Party* tour which effectively ended in the early hours of 3 February 1959^{**} when the plane Holly had chartered crashed, killing all on board in an instant. That most wonderful of faculties hindsight suggests that the accident could possibly have been avoided had the twenty-one year old pilot Roger Peterson been properly warned about the approaching extreme weather conditions, but no amount of harking back makes any difference.

However, as often happens, some good did come out of the tragedy. Even as recently as last year, monies were collected and several music scholarships founded in honour of Holly and the plane's other three occupants. If this doesn't seem too mawkish, there is an intriguing recording of an interview that Norman Petty gave just days after the crash where he comments: 'Who knows why God allows these things to happen, but there has to be a purpose in all of this.'

We do know that the verdict of the US Civil Aeronautics Board announced after several months of investigation was that basic pilot error was to blame and no number of hare-brained theories that have come up over the years can alter that bleak fact.^{***} Upon hearing news of the accident, Buddy's wife, Maria Elena, lost the baby she was carrying, and all his family and

---

[*] Not in the UK of course, where, thanks to the Crickets' recent tour, Holly was a household name, although the Big Bopper had just entered the charts with *Chantilly Lace* and Valens was about to debut with *Donna*.

[**] The old showbusiness adage that the show must go on was not abandoned and the tour limped on with several substitute acts (Frankie Avalon, Jimmy Clanton and — on 3 February, for one night only — a scratch group called the Shadows led by seventeen year old Robert Velline, later Bobby Vee), finally winding up in Springfield, Illinois on 15 February. The remaining Crickets somehow managed to play the remaining thirteen tour dates in a state of shock having been assured that they would be well compensated, but never were.

[***] Most bizarre to this writer is the reasoning that, because Holly carried a pistol with him for protection (he often carried large amounts of cash received from promoters), he may have shot the pilot! Almost as absurd is the alternative suggestion that, because Holly had recently started taking flying lessons, he may have decided to take over the controls of the plane and got into difficulties. Anyone who has read the gruesome detailed official reports will know that neither of these suggested scenarios could possibly be true.

Photo copyright Lew Allen, TM/CMG
Worldwide & Maria Elena Holly.

A frozen-looking Buddy emerges from his tour bus.

friends were obviously devastated by the news.

Under normal circumstances, that should have been the end of things, but to the delight of countless fans Buddy Holly's music wasn't about to just fade away and rose like the proverbial phoenix from the ashes. So much so, that forty years on, when most of his contemporaries are scarcely remembered, his name lingers with a warmth and fondness that suggests it will remain with us for some — perhaps all — of this new Twenty-First Century. Can anything more be asked of an artist in any field? Probably not.

Musical Interlude #7

I Got A Woman, originally recorded by Elvis Presley in January 1956 at the RCA Studios in Nashville.

What'd I Say, recorded by Elvis in August 1963 at Radio Recorders Studio, Los Angeles.

Although Buddy Holly never recorded any Ray Charles material (except for a snippet of *Hallelujah, I Love Her So* taped backstage at a Florida show with Jerry Lee Lewis), there is still an intriguing link with him as revealed below.

It is obvious that Elvis and Buddy were both fans of black music from the outset, and got to hear much of it well before it broke through the racial divide and became fully accepted. Artists like Ray Charles, Lloyd Price, Joe Turner and Fats Domino were long-standing favourites of both singers before most white people had even heard of them.

Although most of Charles' big hits date from the early Sixties (when he topped the US charts with *I Can't Stop Loving You* and *Hit The Road Jack*), he'd actually started recording as far back as 1949 and had struggled for almost a decade to achieve national recognition.

His *I Got A Woman* is a song that Elvis went for in a big way: he performed the gospel-flavoured 1955 R&B chart-topper live on the *Louisiana Hayride* and at numerous concerts throughout his career (usually in medley with *Amen* after August 1971). His version of *What'd I Say* was recorded for the film *Viva Las Vegas* and reached No. 21 in the *Billboard* 'Hot 100' in June 1964.

Whilst Holly was to die even before Brother Ray got to record the seminal *What'd I Say* in 1959, stories from Lubbock tell of him using the radio station speakers there to listen to recordings by Charles, Bo Diddley and others played at full blast.

More significantly, it is known from his widow, Maria Elena, that shortly before his death Holly had tried unsuccessfully to call at Charles' home to discuss the possibility of their collaborating on some material together. This might perhaps explain why half of the dozen numbers Holly left behind on tape at his New York apartment in January 1959 were suited to his style[*], and it may well be that he had been trying out the material in the hope of contacting Ray after the *Winter Dance Party* ended. The numbers included *Drown In My Own Tears*, *Love Is Strange* and *Dearest* and were all songs that one feels could have been worked on successfully in a collaborative way. Of course, we'll never know for certain, and this is yet another of several loose ends that Buddy left behind for others to ponder over.

---

[*] The other half were Buddy's own compositions such as *Learning The Game* and *That Makes It Tough*. It is not known what plans he had for those songs, but we do know that he wanted to bring fellow Texan Terry Noland up to New York to record. Maybe he needed some new material? Of course, all such thoughts are purely speculative.

- CHAPTER 8 -

Did Elvis And Buddy Meet?

The verdict

Before we move on, one small matter needs to be addressed, namely that quote from Elvis mentioned way back in the *Introduction* that he never actually met Buddy Holly. Taken at face value it's a devastating remark that begs some sort of explanation, and a pretty good one at that. Hopefully, from what has been said thus far, most readers will have already formed a view that Elvis' memory must have been playing tricks on him.

It can readily be seen — and is easily verifiable from a network of different sources — that Presley and Holly both shared the same Lubbock stage on several occasions during the course of 1955. In fact, Jerry Allison recently confirmed that 'Buddy and El definitely met. Once, we opened the show for El at Fair Park Coliseum and Buddy borrowed El's guitar'.

If further proof is needed, think also about the settings of those meetings which are described in detail in *Chapter 6* and reflect for a moment. We're not talking here of today's vast concert arenas, but rather about two typical venues in the Fifties set deep in the heart of rural Texas, when to appear together and *not* meet up would have been unthinkable, if not a physical impossibility. Remember too that Elvis wasn't yet some God-like icon insulated from the rest of humanity, but rather an energetic and gregarious young man barely out of his teens.

It's also worth reminding ourselves also that Holly was never billed as a solo act back then but was part of the Buddy & Bob duo/trio who, as a local act, often opened the sort of bills that stars like Elvis or Hank Snow fronted. One thing that is definitely certain is that, at that time, the Texan scarcely resembled the well-groomed singer who later appeared on *American Bandstand* and the *Ed Sullivan Show*. Back in 1955, Holly was still sporting wire-framed specs, Levis, checked shirts and a mouthful of bad teeth. The horn-rims, suits and styled hair were still to come. Even this initial description leads one to suspect that Presley simply didn't recognise the suave chart artist as the young hopeful whom he had met four years earlier during those hectic appearances in 1955. On reflection, maybe it would have been more surprising if he *had* made the connection! Let's pursue these thoughts further. Although increasingly drumming up a storm down South, Presley had not yet acquired the Memphis Mafia entourage or developed the mindset which sadly would isolate him from the outside world and result in him leading the most unorthodox of lives in the ensuing years.

Shortly after being catapulted into the big time, Buddy often mentioned meeting his hero in those early days and there was really no

To whom it may concern

I was shattered to hear of the tragic accident Feb 2 1959 in which Buddy Holly and other members of the Show of Stars 59 were killed. Regarding to my management they'd prepared hundreds of letters. A lot of people asked why I didn't took part at the funeral.

I'd sent a telegram of condolence to the Holleys in Lubbock, Texas in which I confirmed that I was not allowed to leave to took part. The German press is very far behind so they didn't mentioned the plane crash.

I was listening to AFN Frankfurt and after the news John Calder gave me a call and requested an interview. After he talked to my Lt. Col. he decided to call my management. However he'd never gave them a call.

I'd never met Buddy Holly personally but I share the grief with his family and hope that they'll find trust in God as I did after the loss of my beloved mum.

God bless

E.P.

Original text of the 'I'd never met Buddy Holly' letter.

reason for him to invent such comments. Those quotes from radio and television interview transcriptions circa 1957/58 with Red Robinson and others are well documented and if any corroboration were needed Buddy's fellow musicians, Sonny Curtis and Jerry Allison are still around and have confirmed the basic details both to the author and in innumerable interviews down the years.

Not only did they meet, but Allison recalls Buddy teaching Elvis the words to the Drifters' *Money Honey*, which he subsequently performed live in concert and on the *Louisiana Hayride*, and eventually recorded himself a year later.

So, if the case is proven beyond reasonable doubt that Presley's and Holly's paths crossed on several occasions, the only question remaining is the obvious one as to why on earth Elvis should apparently deny the fact?

Let's look firstly at the sad events of February 1959 and remind ourselves of his whereabouts at that time. Buddy had been one of several headliners on an arduous tour of the Midwest, prophetically opening his spot each night with the recent Billy Grammer hit, *Gotta Travel On*: 'Well, I've stayed around, and played around, this old town too long'.

Elvis, meanwhile, was wishing that he still had the opportunity to sing *anywhere* in the United States, but was instead thousands of miles away in Germany 'just rocking and rolling those army tanks' at the behest of Uncle Sam, as he himself so humorously put it in an early interview. He'd been posted there in September 1958 and would remain there until his discharge in March 1960.

It is known that, in the days immediately following the tragic Iowa air crash, Elvis Presley's personal management sent telegrams to the families of the three singers who had lost their lives (Buddy, Holly, the Big Bopper and Ritchie Valens). These were signed 'Private First Class Elvis Presley and Colonel Parker', although they were clearly sent from a location within the USA rather than from Germany.

Buddy's mother (now deceased) remembers receiving such a telegram, while the copy sent to the family of the Big Bopper still exists and is worded: *'We want to extend our heartfelt sympathies to you for the loss you have suffered and our prayers and thoughts are with you in this hour of sorrow.'* Obviously a genuine and sincere thought from one entertainer (or his management, at any rate) to the family of another.

So now we must move on to the mysterious letter which contains the words *'I'd never met Buddy Holly personally'* — an intriguing remark to say the least, given what we know of the events of 1955.

The letter itself didn't actually surface until quite recently, and the heavily-altered copy — reproduced in colour in Andreas Schroer's book, *Private Presley* — is written in black ink and intriguingly opens with *'To Whom It May Concern'*. It is essentially an apologia for failing to attend Buddy's

---

* The accident happened in the early hours of Tuesday, 3 February, while the condolence telegram was dated 5 February. Holly's funeral took place in Lubbock on the following Saturday, 7 February. His friends Bob Montgomery, Jerry Allison, Joe B. Mauldin, Niki Sullivan, Sonny Curtis and Phil Everly acted as pallbearers. Don Everly was too distressed to attend.

funeral on 7 February, but why Presley felt obliged to write it, or precisely who it was intended for, is unclear. He also didn't date it, although it is clear from the content that it was written some time after the event.

Much of the text has been crossed through and alternative wording inserted above. The amendments are in a different, more fluent handwriting and in red ink. It is not known who made the alterations[*], but the rehashed letter is almost as bad at the original and surely could not have been sent out as it stood. Whoever it was, they also helpfully dated the letter (15 February) and noted in the top right-hand corner '*Page 1/1 after Copy*', which appears to confirm that it was intended for publication either as a press release or an open letter to fans. Whether it actually got as far as that remains unconfirmed.

It is interesting that from the early Fifties onwards, when he'd had a scare in a flight over Texas, Presley avoided flying in small planes for the remainder of his life and it's probable that the Holly air-crash reinforced his aversion, as it doubtless did for many other artists of the day. Certainly Jerry Lee Lewis, a friend of Buddy Holly since they toured Australia in 1958, sought to avoid such flights as — ironically — did Eddie Cochran. Presley of course later purchased his own plane, the *Lisa Marie*, but this was a large customised Convair jet which needed four crew and bore more of a similarity to a commercial airliner.

So, in summary, it does seem that Elvis had simply not connected the death of the bespectacled rock & roll singer of *Peggy Sue* fame with the teenaged hillbilly singer he'd encountered four years earlier in rural Lubbock. Remember, if you will, that in 1955 alone he played around 150 shows throughout the southern United States, and those at Lubbock would have been pretty similar to many others in those hectic days. With Buddy and numerous fans and musicians wishing to glad-hand the fast-rising star every time he came into town, it's certainly unsurprising that his recollections after several more equally eventful years may have fogged and merged somewhat.

So, Elvis, we can understand how it was for you back in the Fifties and no apology is needed for the simple slip you made in not connecting the frenetic events of 1955 with the sad ones of early 1959. But you certainly *did* meet Buddy Holly in person, and hopefully that small but important minor musical fact has been settled for all of posterity.

---

[*] Schroer speculates that it was probably Elvis' father, Vernon, but given the latter's known poor literacy skills this seems highly unlikely. A far more likely contender is Elvis' pal, Charlie Hodge. The two had first met in 1956, were inducted into the army together and were subsequently posted to Germany together. Hodge remained 'in service' with Elvis right through to 1977, when he travelled to the hospital with the body.

Musical Interlude #8

Early In The Morning recorded by Buddy Holly at Coral Studios, The Pythian Temple, New York in June 1958.

I'll Be There recorded by Elvis Presley at the American Studios, Memphis in January 1969.

The link between these recordings is again the composer — this time Bobby Darin, another 'great' of the music business who originally wrote and also recorded both numbers himself.

The story of *Early In The Morning* is somewhat convoluted, but in simple terms Darin was signed to Atlantic's Atco subsidiary, hadn't had any hits with them and was going nowhere. Anticipating that he would be released from his contract when it expired later in 1958, he lined up a deal with Decca's Brunswick label and cut the song for them. Life being what it is, however, things did not work out quite as planned.

Against all expectations, *Splish Splash*, a novelty number he had recently recorded, entered the *Billboard* 'Top 100' in June 1958 and shot to No. 3. The follow-up, *Queen Of The Hop*, went nearly as high to No. 9. Atco extended his contract.

In the meantime, Brunswick released *Early In The Morning* credited to a fictitious group, the Ding Dongs. When Atco discovered that the Ding Dongs were actually Darin, they forced Brunswick to hand over the master, which they then re-released on Atco under another contrived name, the Rinky-Dinks. Amazingly, this too was a hit, climbing to No. 24 in the *Billboard* 'Top 100' that summer.

Not to be outdone, Brunswick roped in Buddy Holly (who happened to be in New York at the time) to quickly cut a cover with the same studio musicians that Darin had used. The session included gospel-styled backing from the Helen Way Singers (a black quartet) and a great band which included the respected Panama Francis on drums and Sam 'The Man' Taylor on sax.

So, the world got to hear the Texan on a gospel-sounding number, the result being a hit both in the US and in the UK — No. 32 and No. 17 respectively — with a performance probably as good as any other of his career. Listening to his rendition, it comes as no surprise to learn that Buddy was trying to link up with Ray Charles at the time in the hope of collaborating on some blues or gospel recordings. This again was one of several intriguing and exciting possibilities that were put paid to by the crash that ended his life. (Incidentally, the flip of *Early In The Morning* on the Darin record was another self-composition, *Now We're One*, which Holly also cut for the flip of his single.)

How well Bobby and Buddy knew one another is uncertain, although they had both been headliners on the *Biggest Show Of Stars For 1958* tour that autumn, playing much of the northern USA as well as over the border in Ontario, Canada. Much closer to one another were Bobby and Elvis, as both played extensively in Las Vegas for years and occasionally got to attend each other's shows.

Darin first wrote and recorded *I'll Be There* in 1960 and it was a minor hit for him in the USA that year. Elvis' version was recorded in 1969 and surfaced the following year as a track on the *Let's Be Friends* album, a hotch-potch of film songs and other material that deservedly only reached No. 105 on the *Billboard* 'Top LPs' chart. Curiously, the only act to have a really big hit with the song (on both sides of the Atlantic) was the Liverpool group Gerry & The Pacemakers, in 1965.

Bobby Darin is another major talent that left us much too soon. Aged seven, he had contracted rheumatic fever and suffered irreparable heart damage as a result. He died on 20 December 1973 aged just thirty-seven while undergoing a second bout of open-heart surgery. He had once made himself extremely unpopular by predicting that he would become bigger than Sinatra, a youthful remark he probably later came to regret. Even so, in addition to being a singer, he was also a prolific composer, pianist, drummer, arranger and actor — immensely gifted according to all that knew him. He charted hits from 1958 through to the year of his death, received two Grammy Awards along the way and was nominated for a Hollywood Oscar for his role in *Captain Newman, MD*. Whichever way the scales are weighted, he certainly left an indelible mark on the scene. A few more thoughts are included in the *Glossary*.

- CHAPTER 9 -

Way On Down

Too much

The life of Elvis Presley has already been analysed in a sea of words in the years since his untimely death in 1977, and it's therefore tempting to search for something different to say. Sometimes, events in the life of a subject can become badly distorted with the passage of time — as has so often happened in the past — while that important if elusive ingredient 'truth' can itself so easily become a victim. This has certainly been the case with the fringe literature surrounding Elvis, the passing years fuelling problems as memories continue to fade and falter, while the recent advance of the Internet — with no controlling influence — has further undermined the accuracy of published information on the King.

Sadly, it often seems that ethics were also in short supply in the world of popular music during the Fifties and Sixties, and tales abound of artists who were cheated out of their earnings by a mixture of scheming promoters, record label owners and others who attached themselves to the burgeoning industry. Little wonder that the telling phrase 'If there's a hit, there's a writ' was coined during that era!* Of course, the pendulum has gradually swung back in the opposite direction — so much so that many artists from the decades that followed those early days have literally gone on to earn millions from their activities.

In a major new development, we have also seen attempts to appropriate and 'protect' the image of deceased artists by certain interested parties, and, with the revenues still to be earned from the estates of the likes of Marilyn Monroe, James Dean and others, one can readily understand why this is happening. Of course, we've always known that 'music' and 'business' are really two quite separate words and need to be treated as such if much of the heartache is to disappear.

Hopefully what follows will help to restore some balance through a truthful and fair assessment of Presley's legacy.

Well gather round cats while I tell you a story

We now need to consider the life and music of Elvis Presley using the same parameters as we did for Buddy Holly. What were the milestones that

---

* Unbelievably, Buddy Holly and his co-writers were sued in the 1980s by individuals who claimed they were the original composers of their 1957 smash, *That'll Be The Day*. As the song had been written almost thirty years earlier, the case was dismissed on the grounds that the action had been brought too late.

happened during his life from the tumultuous months of 1955 on through the next twenty-two years that are worthy of repetition and aren't just a rehash of what's been written elsewhere?

Certainly, there's little doubt that Elvis was on a high by the end of 1955 as he finally began to realise his dreams of musical stardom. Despite his lack of national chart success, he'd been voted *Billboard*'s 'Most Outstanding Artist Of 1955' in the country field and had topped a similar deejay poll as 'Best New Male Singer', beating such formidable opponents as Jim Reeves, Porter Wagoner and Bobby Lord.

His parallel dream of a career in films was likewise a tantalising thought, intensified by the release of the new James Dean movie, *Rebel Without A Cause*. It was to become his all-time favourite, and he was soon able to quote much of the dialogue verbatim. In a particularly tragic twist of fate, Dean himself was killed in a car crash that September, just a month before the film's US premiere. Although he never expressed the notion, was there — one wonders — ever in Elvis' mind the dream that, if a screen career materialised, he might somehow fill the void left by Dean's death?

Whatever the speculation, a vision was certainly growing of imminent fame and fortune, and of one thing he was fully convinced: 1956 *had* to be the year that his stage would finally move beyond the confines of the South and embrace all of the then forty-eight states of the USA.

Presley's confidence was well-placed: he clocked up an unprecedented seventeen US hits in 1956, followed by a further nine in 1957, eight in 1958 and four in 1959 — classics like *Heartbreak Hotel, Don't Be Cruel, Hound Dog, Love Me Tender, All Shook Up, Teddy Bear* and *Jailhouse Rock* that established him forever as the King Of Rock & Roll. In the Sixties, he kept up the momentum with equally memorable songs like *Stuck On You, It's Now Or Never, Can't Help Falling In Love, Good Luck Charm* and *Return To Sender*, although the really big hits faded out after 1965's *Crying In The Chapel*.

His film career too had certainly started brightly enough with *Love Me Tender* (1956), *Loving You* (1957), *Jailhouse Rock* (1957), *King Creole* (1958) — all major box office hits — but, although Elvis didn't yet know it, the promising momentum he had built up would soon be lost as a result of the enforced break brought about by his stint in the army, though not through want of trying: between his discharge in 1960 and the end of the decade, he featured in a staggering further twenty-seven movies[*] — that's a rate of almost three a year! Whilst quantity would never be found wanting, quality was a different matter altogether, with only a handful of his earlier efforts proving enduring to anyone other than the staunchest of fans.

After almost a decade of being drip-fed to his public through increasingly drab movies, the King returned to live performance in a big way via December 1968's *Elvis* TV comeback special and continued through the Seventies with a succession of nationwide appearances and Las Vegas residencies. In fact, he was about to embark on yet another tour on the day after his fatal collapse.

---

[*] That abbreviated summary, which ended with his death in August 1977, does not include the two documentary films *Elvis: That's The Way It Is* and *Elvis On Tour* which were made in the early Seventies.

The Colonel and his boy.

There were obviously many other events sandwiched in during those years, but the bulk of the period from 1960 to 1977 was indeed a neverending itinerary of film sets and concert venues. If Elvis looked increasingly tired — with or without the impact of his addiction to pills — perhaps it was with good cause.

It had all seemed so promising back in that exciting year of 1956, when Presleymania broke out all over the USA with the release of *Heartbreak Hotel* and quickly rippled out over the Atlantic to the UK and other distant shores. But even from today's perspective it's not possible to fully analyse why the impact was so great, as the world has since moved on and, as the Eastern saying goes: 'You can never stand in the same river twice'. Putting it another way, it means you can't re-create the past as it always emerges distorted and changed. Thus, whilst recalling odd snippets of days-gone-by from one's own current vantage point can be stimulating for both writer and reader, it can never adequately convey what it was like to be a fan back then, when the sounds were new and the listeners themselves didn't seem to carry so much baggage with them. Life was certainly much simpler then — a fact that most of us would hardly bother to deny.

Why did we callow listeners back then think it was so wonderful to hear the small drawled 'aaahhh' in the middle of Elvis' *That's When Your Heartaches Begin*? Why was the small gasp he made at one point before the phrase 'I'm all shook up' so explosive to the listener? It even seems ludicrous to pose such frivolous questions once the moment has disappeared into the past, but in the Fifties there were hundreds of such small and unique pleasures awaiting the listener as a string of hit records emerged from Elvis Presley and others. It is only in retrospect that we realise we were embarking on a voyage of discovery that would lead to the music and the man still being discussed almost half a century later. Perhaps for many of today's adolescents a similar impact is being created as they listen to *their* idols for the first time, perhaps not. Whilst we're not arguing that the Fifties were totally unique, they *were* a particularly dynamic period given that the world was emerging from the pall that had enveloped it since the 1939–45 war and an explosion of some sort was badly needed, albeit a benign one.

There's another element too that needs to be touched upon. When weighing up Elvis' greatness, some critics harp on about the fact that he composed little of the enormous output of songs he recorded. Indeed, out of seven hundred-plus studio recordings, there were only half-a-dozen titles or so where his name appeared among the composer credits[*] — a mighty small proportion whichever way you slice it. We are then reminded that he was primarily an *entertainer*, a singer of songs, as though this were some minor talent that he shared with very many others. Maybe he was more versatile than most, given the varying styles of music he performed, but not that much more surely? In fact, there *was* quite a bit more to it than that, and millions of fans can testify that Elvis was indeed *very* special.

Surely the point was more about *that voice*, the way he delivered the material and the tremendous energy he generated. Whatever it was, it also had the power to transfer the magic and excitement of his live appearances into those vinyl grooves. Presley's delivery could be decidedly different from song to song, and he used his voice creatively in a way rarely heard in popular music until then. Many tracks could be singled out by way of example, but let's take *Hard Headed Woman* from the late Fifties: the vocal gymnastics he used to convey excitement in the lyrics would look pretty silly if committed to the written page, but they caught the mood of the moment perfectly.

Listening to out-takes of his material nowadays, it can sometimes be heard how he adapted or modified a song on a later take, which at times seems like the work of musical genius. Surely nobody quite like Elvis had come along before with such an innovative talent.

Given these facts, it's always seemed somewhat harsh to expect Elvis to have been a multi-instrumentalist and a songwriter in addition to his other talents! Why do we yearn for such all-round perfection from our musical idols, from the sportsmen, actors and others who entertain us down to the politicians and statesmen who attempt to represent and govern us? Is it that their lives have to be exemplary so as to contrast with our own more humdrum existences?

Once again we've digressed. We are still in the Fifties and the voyage of discovery for the listener would continue as, after the initial recordings, we witnessed the dynamism of those first screen appearances and later still heard Elvis being interviewed. Here, perhaps somewhat surprisingly, we discovered a funny, thoughtful and intelligent man far removed from the stereotype portrayed by the media then as now.

---

[*] The best known of these must be *Heartbreak Hotel* and *Don't Be Cruel*, which certainly weren't Presley's own compositions, although in interpreting them he definitely added new dimensions to what the original composers set down on paper. Other titles included joint compositions with his long-time pal from schooldays, Red West, but it remains open to debate how much each man actually contributed to their creation. There is, however, a lengthy list of songs which were not written by Elvis, but which he either adapted or arranged.

Backstage in Canada, April 1957.

Uncle Sam wants YOU!

To disappear from the music scene in 1958 after his conscription into the army must have seemed like the end of the line for Elvis, given that his career had hit an amazing plateau of success that year. To eventually re-emerge two years later and simply pick up where he left off was an incredible achievement that surely can't be explained away merely by citing Colonel Tom Parker's manipulations and shrewd shenanigans. The public, who can usually sense when an artist has feet of clay, are equally adept at appreciating real talent — which perhaps explains why some performers can get by without a hit record for decades and still enjoy long-term careers. Perhaps that's what helped Elvis to so effortlessly retain his formidable fanbase

Fellow GI Buddy Knox visits Elvis at his rented home in Fort Hood, Texas.

during that lengthy absence? Meanwhile, it had seemed more than likely that someone else from all the emerging talent — perhaps Jerry Lee Lewis — might come along to replace the singer in the public's affection during this time. Tempting as it is to speculate, for whatever reasons it just didn't happen.

Yet another book (*Private Presley*, the one containing the condolence letter) has dissected the period Elvis spent as US Army Private 53 310 761 in Germany and his determination to serve his country as a regular GI, even if he did work himself up to buck sergeant before his stint was through.

There's not too much mystery about this period. For instance, it is well known that he first met his future wife Priscilla Beaulieu over there, and it was probably inevitable from early on that they would one day marry even if it wasn't articulated to the outside world. It is equally well known that, just weeks before he embarked for the former West Germany on the troop ship *USS General Randall* for his eighteen-month tour of duty, his beloved mother died unexpectedly at the age of forty-six — an event that had a devastating effect on him as he tried to complete his army service while at the same time also trying to support his father Vernon in their shared grief.

As far as his career in music went, Elvis never saw the inside of a recording studio for almost two whole years from the day he set sail for Germany in mid-1958, his many releases throughout this period being drawn from material that RCA had stockpiled prior to his departure. On the movie front, the already-completed *King Creole* was held back several months and not released until his army career was well underway.

Interestingly, the many private home recordings that have surfaced from those army days confirm what Presley's general musical tastes were at the time, sung as they were for relaxation or enjoyment and with no indication that the material was being worked on for possible release. Play them, and one instantly feels there's scant regard on the part of the singer as to what

posterity might think, and little or no pretentiousness. The songs — it's probably fairer to call them 'amateur recordings' — are an eclectic mix of religious tunes, standards, country songs and ballads, and the only real surprise is the lack of any blues-styled numbers amongst them.

Despite the successes he enjoyed following his discharge from the army, it's an undisputed fact that Elvis' career began to stagnate in the mid-to-late Sixties once the honeymoon period that his initial return evoked had subsided. The British Invasion led by the Beatles ran almost parallel with his continuing film career, and the energy they and others brought to the music scene only served to underscore the extent to which he was becoming marooned in a veritable lagoon of repetitious, lightweight musical pap.

Tom Jones vividly remembers talking to Elvis around that time and genuinely feels his own Las Vegas success at this juncture helped him to realise that he needed to return to live performance again and reach out physically to his fans, rather than just appearing before them as a fleeting image on a screen. He'd just made a sensational comeback via December 1968's *Elvis* TV special, so why not get back on stage big time — and if so, where better than in that showbusiness Mecca, Vegas?

Sin City, here I come

There's no doubt that Elvis enjoyed plenty of success between 1956 and the late Sixties, although by 1968 his career — while not exactly in free-fall — had certainly reached a low point. Something was definitely needed to inject new life and 1969 was to be the year, although it is unclear who should be given the credit for the relaunch. The plain fact was that the Swinging Sixties were ebbing away — they hadn't swung that much for Elvis anyway — and his career desperately needed to move forward after such a long, directionless period.

After completing *The Trouble With Girls*, the last of his conveyor-belt movies for M-G-M[*], he finally got the chance to tackle a project with some substance. Certainly, with Universal's *Change Of Habit*, Presley portrayed a markedly different image and the film had a real dose of social awareness which, with the help of his co-star Mary Tyler-Moore, should have given it the extra lift that was needed. In the event, it did do reasonable business at the box office, being ranked 14th highest grossing film of the year in the US, but ultimately it was just too little being offered too late to bring about any real change.

Certainly no-one could complain that Elvis was lazy, and the year was a particularly busy one for him. Apart from shooting the aforementioned films, he also restarted his long association with Las Vegas[**] with fifty-seven

---

[*] Ironically, M-G-M has followed Elvis into history and is no longer known for films, having sold its studio lot and moved into the world of hotels.

[**] The first shows Elvis ever gave in Vegas were, of course, back in the days of the Elvis Presley Trio when they had appeared in early 1956 at a place called the New Frontier to a reception that was decidedly less than enthusiastic — as live recordings from the dates testify. The premature curtailment of this booking was the only major setback he endured during that otherwise hugely successful year.

Lookin' good at the 'Elvis: That's The Way It Is' rehearsals, summer 1970.

consecutive appearances that summer at the International (later renamed the Hilton) to standing-room-only business. Whether he was inspired by Tom Jones' suggestion we'll never know for sure, but he was definitely on the way back and would never really go away again.

It was around this period too that Tim Rice included the word 'superstar' in the title of his new musical based on the life of Jesus Christ* and the hybrid word soon attached itself to Elvis, becoming an obvious way to raise his status above the other stars of the day. It certainly caught on and it was soon to be followed by the next rung on the ladder of hype: megastar. Such terms are probably used much too liberally today, although most would accept that Elvis was one of the few popular artists to actually merit such hyperbole.

One of the saddest aspects of Presley's Seventies' renaissance has to be that the image of Elvis and Las Vegas would eventually become synonymous — an association that still persists to the present day, despite the fact that (according to his confidante, Larry Geller) the singer hated the gamblers' playground and always referred to it as 'Sin City'.

---

* The Andrew Lloyd-Webber and Tim Rice musical, *Jesus Christ Superstar* premiered in 1972, arousing considerable controversy for coupling the name of the Son of God with such an irreverent term.

All my trials, Lord

The sequence of events enumerated under this heading shouldn't have been a problem for a rich, handsome and talented person like Elvis Presley, but perhaps each man really is an island and we shouldn't confuse the image the outside world sees with how the individual inwardly perceives himself. Was there something within his psyche which gnawed away at him and finally caused him to implode from around 1972 onwards when his relationship with Priscilla began to unravel? A failed marriage with or without a child is not something to be lightly shrugged off by anyone, although it's painfully close to being par for the course for many people these days. However, the only fallout that most experience is some sadness and heartache, but rarely anything that becomes life-threatening. With Elvis, a malaise seems to have set in which ultimately contributed towards his early demise — even if many of those closest to him either couldn't see beyond the image or were powerless to intervene.

There were many other factors, of course. The main one was undoubtedly his medically-sanctioned narcotics habit, whilst the unreal world that he had created around himself cannot exactly have helped his constitution and well-being however much it had become his 'normal' way of life.

Although Presley continued to do remarkable business in Vegas — he never played to an empty seat — his concert appearances there became predictable to the point where (Paul Simon humorously recalls) every song finished with an explosion and a karate chop! Maybe that wasn't literally what happened, as the fans still loved him, but there certainly was little challenge or incentive there for the singer. Somehow or other, Elvis' career once again became bogged down in a sameness that may have been acceptable to his audiences but failed to give him the stimulation he needed so badly. Listening today to those live recordings from the Vegas years, the amount of duplication that abounds in the playlists is striking, although it must also be acknowledged that he also recorded some of his most challenging and revealing material — such as the achingly introspective *Walk A Mile In My Shoes* — during this period.

If the picture emerging at this time is one of a sad individual, many accounts of those that were close to Elvis build up a quite different portrait. For example, J.D. Sumner, leader of the Stamps quartet, remembers him as one of the happiest men he had ever met, and said he couldn't recall a single day in the life of Elvis that hadn't been filled with laughter! Perhaps that's pushing credulity somewhat, as the consensus points towards something having gone very wrong, even if we disregard the evidence of Presley's failing health.

It's a fact that, for the last couple of years of his life, it was almost an impossibility to get him into the recording studio, although producer Felton Jarvis and others tried — and this from someone who had lived most of his life simply to make music. Many sensed that something wasn't quite right, even if what to do about it was another question. 'Much too late to help Elvis' was the dubious warning that two former long-time members of his entourage, Sonny and Red West (together with Dave Hebler), published as *Elvis: What Happened?* just days before his fatal collapse.

The strain begins to show, 1975.

From Graceland to the Promised Land

Although we're talking of a sad time, the title of Merle Haggard's 1977 tribute album to the King following his shock death on 16 August is too good not to re-use as a heading for this section. It really says it all, and the earnest if mawkish wish of every real fan must be that Elvis did find some reward at the end — even if the image of him dying in solitude on the toilet conjures up a scene of dreadful pathos. It was certainly a most unfitting end for one of the most electrifying and charismatic performers the world has ever known.

The film footage of Elvis waiting in the wings to go onstage for one of the final concerts, hugely overweight and trying to smile for the camera is almost as haunting. In fact, in some ways it's a relief to think that he didn't have to embark upon yet another gruelling concert tour which the Colonel had already lined up for that August and for which he was forlornly trying to get fit with the odd bout of racketball. Forty-two is in some ways a very young age, but Elvis really had lived his life in fast-forward and maybe had achieved all that he was going to, given the way his life had unfolded. In retrospect, perhaps it isn't totally surprising that he died that August.

That fans and other visitors still flock to Graceland a quarter of a century later is a tribute to the man and his music, and the mark he made during his time on Earth. He was certainly more than just another entertainer, and, in describing his death, US President Jimmy Carter eulogised that America had lost a part of itself, and that the singer had symbolised 'the vitality, rebelliousness and good humor' of his nation.

Any eulogy should also be able to take comfort in the fact that, in a relatively long career, Elvis got to sing music from such a broad spectrum of genres — from country to R&B, soul to outright pop, and from the secular to gospel and the seasonal fare of his hit Christmas recordings.

Of course, today's generation doesn't necessarily thrill to Presley's image just as most of us couldn't get too excited by that of Rudolph Valentino and his contemporaries from yesteryear. Fashions inevitably change, and the poses of many of today's idols will doubtless likewise look foolish in the years to come. There's a real impermanence about the world and its artefacts that the turn of the century has only added to, although it does nobody any harm to muse upon this fact.

There's many an anonymous epithet that can summarise a life, and it was Dr. Martin Luther King who famously reflected that longevity in itself need not be the yardstick. More recently, the late BBC broadcaster Brian Redhead opined that 'Life is not chronological but theological'. Many other sayings with a similar theme could also be quoted, such as the archetypal gravestone that reads:

> *Laugh not at me as you pass by*
> *As you are now, so once was I*
> *As I am now, so shall you be*
> *Prepare for death and follow me.*

An unknown maxim that the author came across while working on this book would seem to particularly reflect many of the facets of Elvis' personality and is also worth repeating: *'Think deeply, speak gently, love much, laugh often, work hard, give freely and be kind'*. Elvis certainly didn't get everything right in his life, but most of the above phrases are echoed by many of those who knew him along the way. If, as it seems, we all strive to leave behind a mark in the sand after our departure from this world, then Elvis Presley for one surely did.

---

* It's also interesting to contrast how much public tastes changed over the eighteen years between Holly's death and Presley's. When Buddy died in 1959, a rash of tribute discs like Mike Berry's *Tribute To Buddy Holly*, Tommy Dee's/Ruby Wright's *Three Stars*, Benny Barnes' *Gold Records In The Snow*, etc appeared — all maudlin teenybopper efforts very much in the *Tell Laura I Love Her* fictional 'death disc' style of the day. By 1977, however, the vogue for such corny paeans had evaporated and the King was commemorated rather more tastefully — and over a more respectable period — through recordings such as Dire Straits' reflective *Calling Elvis* from 1991 and, coincidentally from the same year, singer-songwriter Marc Cohn's *Walking In Memphis*.

Musical Interlude #9

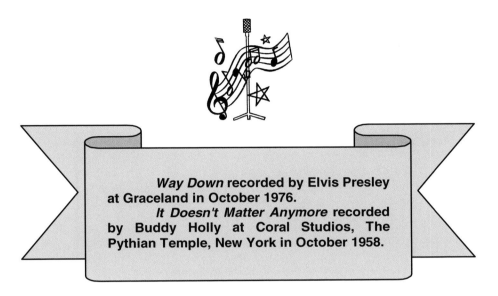

Way Down recorded by Elvis Presley at Graceland in October 1976.
It Doesn't Matter Anymore recorded by Buddy Holly at Coral Studios, The Pythian Temple, New York in October 1958.

The connection here is the peculiar, possibly slightly spooky one that when a singer makes a tragic exit from this world their last recording is invariably one that only serves to point up the total irony of the tragedy. Furthermore the fault can't necessarily be laid at the feet of the record company in question, however cynical these institutions sometimes appear. But random chance surely cannot be to blame either, and one wonders whether someone up there is pulling the strings and inviting the Grim Reaper to come along with his bony grin and give a thumbs up to the record being a hit.

Elvis usually steered clear of songs that had too much of a presentiment about them, but despite this recorded *Way Down* in late 1976 as one of four tracks at his final session in the Jungle Room at Graceland. With the inference in the lyrics that the singer is about to visit places he hasn't been before, the spectre of death is certainly felt throughout the record — albeit perhaps with an element of hindsight given that it was nestling in the charts when he himself passed away in August 1977.

The circumstances surrounding Holly's offering were even more macabre. Buddy was at what would turn out to be his final studio session in New York cutting four pre-selected numbers when his friend Paul Anka rushed in at the last moment clutching the lyrics to a song he'd just written for him, *It Doesn't Matter Anymore*. Hindsight indicates that a more ironic title would be hard to invent. And so the Reaper once again managed to gatecrash the proceedings and get the last chuckle.

The roll call of other artists who recorded songs with similar overtones is legion: from Hank Williams (*I'll Never Get Out Of This World Alive*) to the much-missed Eddie Cochran (*Three Steps To Heaven*) to the great Chuck Willis — a particular favourite of both Elvis & Buddy — whose prophetic double-sided posthumous hit, *What Am I Living For* b/w *Hang Up My Rock & Roll Shoes* is one of the classic examples of the genre. Country artist Hawkshaw Hawkins (who perished along with Patsy Cline and Cowboy Copas when their plane ploughed into the side of a hill in 1963) managed to put a poignant twist on things with *Sunny Side Of The Mountain*, his first as well as his last hit. Patsy likewise conformed to type, her recording of *Leavin' On Your Mind* having just dropped off the charts at the time of the fatal accident. Not to be outdone, Copas also got in on the act with his first posthumous release — ironically titled *Goodbye Kisses* — which likewise went straight into the charts.

Did Otis Redding perhaps anticipate a watery grave when he recorded *(Sitting On The) Dock Of The Bay* in December 1967 — three days before his plane nose-dived into Lake Monona, Wisconsin en route to an engagement in the Midwest, killing him and most of his backing band, the Bar-Kays? It was his own composition and far and away the most wistful-sounding record he'd ever made. What had led him to pen such a song that was so out of character, and who can possibly explain such things? The cynic would of course instantly dismiss any explanation that couldn't be tested under laboratory conditions, while others might be less dogmatic and perhaps agree that there might be some things in heaven and earth that we just don't understand and probably never will.

Of course, the phenomenon of prophetic titles didn't stop in the Sixties, and since then artists such as Marvin Gaye and John Lennon have also managed to cut seemingly doom-laden material shortly before their unexpected deaths. Similarly, some groups have gone out of their way to tempt providence further by giving themselves names such as 'the Grateful Dead' or 'Nirvana', but that's another story and a cul-de-sac we'll avoid going down here.

For anyone who hasn't already overdosed on this particular section, the book *Death Discs* by Alan Clayson is strongly recommended, containing as it does nearly every known permutation concerning all things morbid within — and sometimes without — the realms of Tin Pan Alley. Why, he even points out that ex-Yardbird's Keith Relf's last demo before he sadly accidentally electrocuted himself was *All The Falling Angels*!

But how about another example from each of our main subjects to finish off this theme? Could anything possibly top 'That'll be the day when I die' — the lyrical hook from Holly's self-penned first hit, containing (with due hindsight) the ultimate in fatalistic overtones? Possibly only the fact that the very last studio track Elvis ever recorded was, believe it or not, *He'll Have To Go*!

---

[*] Her earlier hit, *I Fall To Pieces*, coincided with her being hospitalised following a car crash!

- CHAPTER 10 -

Linked Lives? Linked Destinies?

Alan Mann with Christine Leveridge, MAA

Two seeds from the same cotton patch

Whatever yardstick is used to measure the impact of Elvis Presley and Buddy Holly the same conclusion is reached, namely that, at its simplest, they both lived astonishing yet contrasting lives in their given sphere and went on to influence countless others during a lifetime of spectacular achievement. This would appear to be a truism, whether their lives are judged immediately following their early demise or in retrospect over the ever-lengthening years that have followed (that's forty-three and counting for Buddy, while for Elvis the significant quarter century milestone will have passed by the time these words are read). In neither case has the passage of time dimmed their achievements, rather each of their lives can be looked back on with an increasing sense of wonder. If hindsight and passing years do little to tarnish the legend, then the converse — that time has only added to the lustre — would surely be easier to argue.

That the paths of these two musical giants crossed several times during their careers should maybe come as no great surprise — they were after all close contemporaries — but it is amazing to contemplate that they may have been somehow linked by destiny from the moment of their births. And, if that premise is accepted, would it not follow that their souls are also inextricably bound up, even if that conjures up the momentary vision of a heavenly supergroup acquiring two new members!

Naturally, readers will have their own set of beliefs and can decide for themselves whether what happened in each of their lives was pre-ordained or whether, the pieces of the jigsaw having been tossed into the air, each of them then somehow neatly fell into its allotted place. This of course then begs the most mysterious question of all, whether we as humans really have free will during our brief lives, or whether what we are and what we achieve during the course of our lifetimes simply forms part of some predetermined grand plan.

You will be relieved to know that such profundities are well outside the scope of the present book, even supposing the author had the wit to comment. But anyone reading thus far will have guessed that I have no personal doubts that both singers had a destiny to work through, irrespective of whether they — or any of us — have any insight at all into the bigger picture.

You may remember my mentioning in the *Personal Prologue* that the genesis of this publication came about by chance when I stumbled upon an astrology book which described Elvis and Buddy (or more correctly any two individuals who shared their particular birth dates) as peas in a pod with strong bonds that have an almost fatalistic or karmic cast to them.

Rather than pin everything on the revelations of that solitary work, I decided to enlist the help of a professional astrologer in the hope that this additional research might amplify or at the very least verify what I had come across. Far from demolishing the notion of any sort of cosmic link between the two men (a worst-case scenario I was willing to face philosophically), Christine Leveridge's comparative analysis of their respective horoscopes was a revelation.

Her findings are presented a little later in this chapter, but to set the scene we must again briefly reflect upon how rock & roll itself magically sprang into being and in doing so launched the careers of a generation of musical hopefuls including the two subjects of this book.

Was it really all just coincidence?

Over the years, many thousands of words have been written on the origins of rock & roll and its Southern sidekick, rockabilly, with no two experts ever quite agreeing as to the detail. It seems to have simply exploded without warning, like the mythical Atlantis re-emerging from the depths, then faded out just as quickly a few years later leaving in its wake the ubiquitous 'rock music', an all-embracing term that remains with us through to the present day. Or was the so-called 'El Niño effect' (when a butterfly flaps its wings thousands of miles away, a tidal wave arrives somewhere else) involved in its inception, and if so, where precisely did that first tiny tremor come from, and did it break off from the stem of country music, the blues or elsewhere?

Depending on which expert one defers to, it may not have been a complicated fusion at all but simply country music shedding its skin and absorbing the black rhythms, or conversely black music absorbing contemporary country sounds and finally bursting free from its minority audiences to land centre stage.

Rock & roll may have been the ultimate in hybrid offspring, but it surely does no harm to reflect on the wonders of its birth. Who, for instance, can explain why so many of the genre's giants (Holly, Presley, Jerry Lee Lewis, Little Richard, Carl Perkins, Johnny Cash and Wanda Jackson, to briefly cherry-pick) were all born within the space of a few years during the 1930s, and within such a relatively tiny sector of the Southern USA? Isn't it remarkable that these individuals seemed to suddenly spring up so close to one another with such energy to fuse those musical strands into such a vibrant new form of music?

Maybe American Indian ancestry had something to do with it. Isn't it ironic that, having almost been wiped off the face of the North American continent by the white man, those downtrodden (and spiritual) people should have surfaced again so creatively in art and in music during the last century? That some of the most sensitive of all singers — Elvis, Buddy, Marty Robbins, Johnny Cash, Waylon Jennings, Johnny Horton, Charlie Feathers and perhaps the 'missing link' to rock & roll, Johnnie Ray himself — should share such a heritage is surely no simple coincidence.

Given the vastness of the United States, what extraordinary force was it that drove the paths of Elvis Presley and Buddy Holly to cross in, of all places, Lubbock, Texas — little more than a pinprick on the map — and subsequently decreed that Elvis should have to constantly drive from his Memphis home to *Holly*wood through the Texas Panhandle just a few miles away from the cemetery where Buddy Holly lies buried? And was it just pure chance that the filming of the *Buddy Holly Story* biopic commenced within weeks of Elvis' death in August 1977?

Astral buddies

Not many people earn millions of dollars after their death as well as having stage shows continuously touring the world in their memory, but as any one of their millions of fans will tell you, Elvis and Buddy were unique. This fact is confirmed by the unusual planetary configurations in their birth charts, as one might expect of men who have reached such pinnacles of success, as indeed are their character similarities and basic compatability. Their Moon signs, for instance (Pisces for Elvis, Gemini for Buddy) indicate that there was far more to each of them than was apparent from their public personas.

True to his name, Elvis (the 'all-wise') was considerably more intelligent and contemplative than suggested by the laid-back, affable image he presented to interviewers. It is well documented that he knew it was his destiny to become world-famous and subsequently spent a significant part of his life in a spiritual quest to discover why he had been put on this earth.

Buddy, on the other hand, was intensely ambitious, belying the mild exterior he exhibited to the outside world. Because of this powerful hidden drive, it is likely that he would have achieved prominence whatever section of society he was born into. As those who knew him well will readily confirm, he was nowhere near as shy and retiring as he appeared.

Aspects and chart placements to Mercury (planet of the mind, numbers and basic education) indicate that both men were intelligent and lively social animals. Both started school during the Second World War, absorbing similar values and culture, and both had hidden talents. Buddy was certainly more intelligent than his meagre academic achievements imply, whilst Elvis was drawn towards numbers and later in fact became a gifted numerologist.

They were most definitely karmically linked, with Elvis' Sun sign, Capricorn, making a trine (an excellent aspect) to Buddy's Virgo; their natal Moons were both in Mutable signs; and Buddy's Ascendant (Capricorn) was conjunct with Elvis' Sun. This latter aspect is found in very successful marriages and business partnerships, so it's very disappointing that they never linked up again after the mid-Fifties — they could have made beautiful music together.

These and other aspects also indicate that Elvis and Buddy thought alike, felt similarly about things, and had the same motivation in life as

Natal chart for Elvis Presley

Source of birth data: Birth certificate and the Astrological Association of Great Britain.

Birth date	8 January 1935
Birth time	4:35:00 am
TG	CST

Birth place	East Tupelo, MS
Longitude	88° 43' W
Latitude	34° 16' N

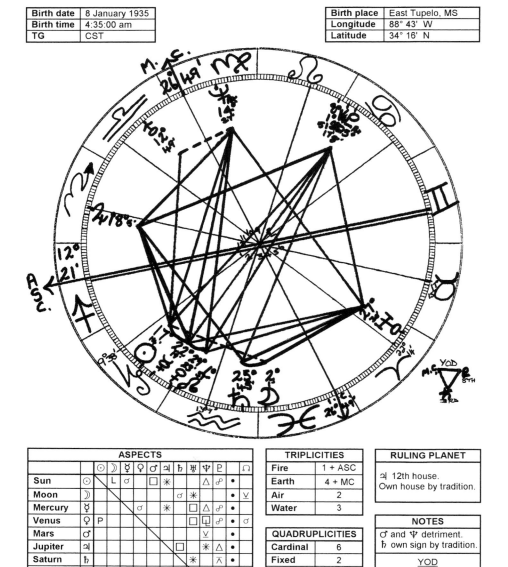

ASPECTS

		☉	☽	☿	♀	♂	♃	♄	♅	♆	♇		☊
Sun	☉		L	♂		□	✶			△	⚼	•	
Moon	☽					♂	✶			•	⌄		
Mercury	☿				♂	✶		□	△	⚼	•		
Venus	♀	P					□	⊡	⚼	•	♂		
Mars	♂								⌄	•			
Jupiter	♃						□		✶	△	•		
Saturn	♄							✶		⋏	•		
Uranus	♅								⊡	□	•	□	
Neptune	♆									•			
Pluto	♇									•	♂		
	☊	•	•	•	•	•	•	•	•	•	•		
ASC					✶			⊡	□				
MC				△	△			⋏	⋏		✶		

TRIPLICITIES

Fire	1 + ASC
Earth	4 + MC
Air	2
Water	3

QUADRUPLICITIES

Cardinal	6
Fixed	2
Mutable	2

Positive	3
Negative	7

☊☋	1° 4' ≈

RULING PLANET

♃ 12th house.
Own house by tradition.

NOTES

♂ and ♆ detriment.
♄ own sign by tradition.

YOD
MC
♄ 3rd △ ♅ 5th

CARDINAL T □
♈ ☉ — ♋
☿ ♀ — ♇
♅ ♈

© 2002 Christine Leveridge, 12 Uplands Avenue, Clayton Heights, Queensbury, W. Yorks BD13 1EN

Natal chart for Buddy Holly

Source of birth data: Mrs. Ella Holley and the Astrological Association of Great Britain.

Birth date	7 September 1936
Birth time	3:30:00 pm
TG	CST

Birth place	Lubbock, TX
Longitude	101° 51' W
Latitude	33° 35' N

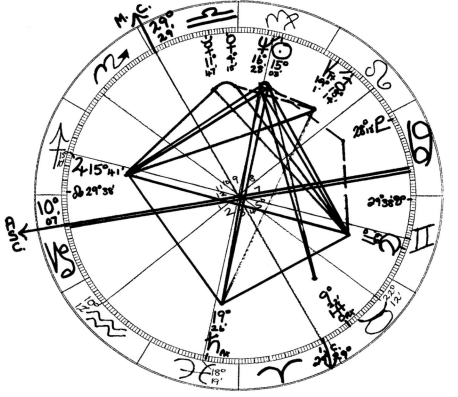

ASPECTS												
	☉	☽	☿	♀	♂	♃	♄	♅	♆	♇		☊
Sun	☉	□				□	☍	△	♂	L	•	
Moon	☽			△	△		☍	□		□	L	•
Mercury	☿				♂	*						•
Venus	♀					L					•	□
Mars	♂						△	⊼		⋁	•	
Jupiter	♃							□		□	•	
Saturn	♄			P					♂		•	
Uranus	♅									△	•	
Neptune	♆	P									•	
Pluto	♇			P							•	⊼
		•	•	•	•	•	•	•	•	•	•	
	☊											
ASC		△	⊼	□	□			△	△			
MC		L					L		L	L	□	

TRIPLICITIES	
Fire	2
Earth	3 + ASC
Air	3 + MC
Water	2

QUADRUPLICITIES	
Cardinal	3
Fixed	2
Mutable	5

Positive	5
Negative	5

☊☋ 0° 26' ♑

RULING PLANET

♄ 3rd house.

NOTES

MUTABLE
GRAND CROSS

♐ ♃		☉ ♆ ♍
12th		8th
♄ ♓		☽ ♊
3rd		5th

♃ and ♀ own sign.
♆ detriment.

© 2002 Christine Leveridge, 12 Uplands Avenue, Clayton Heights, Queensbury, W. Yorks BD13 1EN youngsters towards their musical careers. The mid-points and harmonics in their respective birth charts provide further confirmation that when they did meet up, they were friends and, given more time together, would have been very close. They were both determined boys from relatively poor backgrounds, and their charts show that it was no accident that they were both drawn to the most revolutionary music of the time, rock & roll. Of course, it helped that both had parents who demonstrably loved them and supported them wholeheartedly from the beginning.

Before the planet Neptune was discovered, Jupiter, the largest planet in our Solar System, traditionally had rulership of the twelfth house of the horoscope. Elvis and Buddy both have Jupiter placed in early degrees of the twelfth house. This positioning brings glorious rewards to the hard-working, and both certainly drove themselves — and the musicians with whom they worked — extremely hard. It also inspires a confidence that 'everything will be all right' and must have helped considerably in their ambitions to become chart-toppers against such immense competition.

Subjects with a twelfth house Jupiter are known for their generosity, often through donations to charity. Elvis, of course, was incredibly generous and Buddy's chart likewise indicates that, had he lived longer, he too would have been one of life's givers.

Additionally, Jupiter's influence in both men's horoscopes is accentuated by the fact that it is Elvis' chart ruler and Buddy has the planet placed in its own sign. What these two men had in common was not just good music; they both tuned into a higher vibration very much in harmony with the planets to create a completely new kind of music, a music for young people, a music with mass appeal, a music that would last forever.

Rather more poignantly, Jupiter (the planet of dreams, fantasy, imagination, escapism and glamour) also rules drugs and air travel. In Elvis' case, his twelfth house Jupiter squares Saturn, eroding his stability; in Buddy's case, his natal Jupiter makes negative aspects to several other planets in his chart.

It's also interesting to note that Elvis and Buddy also both had Venus (the planet of love, money and marriage) in cardinal signs, the 'movers and shakers' of the Zodiac. Elvis' Venus in Capricorn and the planetary aspects it makes indicates that he actually had fewer physical relationships with women than publicised, whilst Buddy, whose Venus was in Libra was rather more of a charmer and ladies' man than is universally known. Perhaps it's as well that we're reading all of this with hindsight!

During their lifetimes, both their wives were vilified — Priscilla for her extreme youth when she first went to live at Graceland, Maria Elena because she was Puerto Rican and a different religion from Buddy. After their deaths, both displayed a flair for business acumen, with Priscilla just having the edge (women will often fight harder for their offspring than on their own behalf).

More controversially, it can also be deduced that both artists were also architects of their own demise[*]: Holly by deciding to fly in atrocious wintry

---

[*] Coincidentally, Buddy was born on a Monday and died on a Monday night/Tuesday morning, while Elvis was born on a Tuesday and died on a Tuesday.

conditions so that he could get his laundry done (a typical clean and tidy Virgo!), Presley through his excessive drug-taking. The overwhelming impression left by both their deaths is their sheer pointlessness.

The conditions for the phenomenal success these two artists enjoyed were created by Pluto, the outermost planet of the solar system, which is connected to getting money from other people leading to corporate wealth, death and regeneration. The way in which they remained popular and continued to earn vast sums even after their deaths is characteristic of its influence.

Because it takes some 250 years to complete a full transit of the twelve signs of the Zodiac, it is regarded by astrologers as a generational planet. At birth, Elvis and Buddy both had Pluto placed in the final degrees of Cancer. In this position, Pluto denoted the scattering of relatives. Indeed, economic hardships of the Depression resulted in massive population movements within the United States, but there were also other enormous social changes in the Twenties and Thirties. As travel became increasingly sophisticated, more and more people began moving away from their home towns and away from their families. The telephone began to assume increasing importance as a means of communication.

In August 1938, Pluto moved into glamorous Leo — in which sign its effects are 'exalted' (intensified). The following two decades witnessed an unprecedented explosion within the music and radio industries that was mirrored by equally dramatic developments in the world of film and television. Recently invented colour processes gave film-makers the opportunity to create fantasy worlds and spectacle on a scale never before seen. The miracle of the small screen broke down social barriers by giving millions of ordinary people access to the lives of the rich and famous: for the first time ever, they could see what they were doing and how they lived. Other barriers disappeared as black music was gradually accepted by white people and vice versa. Music provided fodder for radio and television's voracious appetite. One movie or TV appearance (even if only from the waist up) could generate many thousands of dollars in record sales. Small wonder, then, that the world suddenly became populated with so many film stars, pop stars and TV stars.

So what was it that made Elvis and Buddy so unique? The answer lies in the stars: they were both born at very special moments in time and place.

Numbered days?

It seems to me a strange coincidence that the years 1959 and 1977 have in common much more than the deaths of Buddy Holly and Elvis Presley, albeit that those single events alone were enough to blow gaping holes in the popular music firmament. It is of course axiomatic that, for every year that passes, a never-ending stream of musical figures shrug off this mortal coil, but by any yardstick 1959 and 1977 surely stand out more in the memory than any other year in the last half-century. In both cases, it somehow seemed as if their deaths were a catalyst for other events that went on to shake the entertainment world within the space of just a few months.

It's surely no accident that the dates '1959' and '1977' both reduce down to the number 6, such a heavy resonance in the field of numerology. It is, for example, the first absolutely perfect number as defined by the Greek mathematician, Euclid. (To be precise, the factors of 6 are 1, 2 and 3 — no other numbers divide into 6 — and when added together they also total 6!) The fact that God is said to have created the perfection of our world in just 6 days, and juxtaposed, that Christ died on the cross at the 6th hour all pointed the ancient world to revere the number and attach huge meaning to it. This special number is also apparent within the natural world in the hexagonal structure of the snowflake and the honeycomb of the bee, while the music world has the hexachord — the diatonic series of six notes with a semitone between the third and the fourth. So, there is a definite thought that the years we're discussing here are of particularly great significance, even if tragically so.

Anyone who has read thus far will be more than familiar with the death of Buddy Holly and his co-stars in the depths of wintry Iowa in February 1959, but it is only infrequently recalled that, five months later, Billie Holiday — probably the world's greatest female jazz singer — also departed forever at the age of just forty-four after a life sadly blighted and foreshortened by drugs. This was followed by an even greater shock in October 1959, when the then most popular classical tenor in history, Mario Lanza, died prematurely at the even younger age of thirty-eight.

Even if none of the intervening years approached the tragedies of 1959, 1977 again confirmed the adage that bad luck comes in threes, as the sudden demise of Elvis Presley from heart failure at the age of forty-two heralded another triple blow to the world of popular entertainment. One month later to the day, a late-night car crash claimed the life of thirty-year old Marc Bolan**, while October saw the passing of popular music's first superstar, Bing Crosby, at the age of seventy-four.

Although the years before and since have witnessed other tragedies, never have the groupings been more potent than in 1959 and 1977.

Moreover, wasn't it ironic that Buddy Holly's death at the age of 22 (there's that 22 again!) was shoehorned numerically between the death of his great friend, Eddie Cochran (21) and that of the singer who most wanted to be like him but only lived a year longer, Bobby Fuller (23). And how curious that Elvis Presley (42) should have died one year after the singer who was perhaps his greatest acolyte, Ral Donner (41), and a year before the 'Australian Elvis', Johnny O'Keefe (43).

The mention of such numerical coincidences will doubtless leave some readers unconvinced, but as the old maxim says: if to the believer no proof is necessary, then to the sceptic no proof is possible. Let's move on.

---

* It's tempting to delve much deeper than the rather brief mention of numerology made in this chapter. For example, the number 11 is considered a master vibration, and with this thought in mind I looked into Buddy Holly's first great solo hit, *Peggy Sue*. Would you believe that it entered the US *Billboard* 'Top 100' chart on *11* November 1957? Analyse that sequence and it becomes 11.11.1957 (1+9+5+7=22!). I need hardly add that the record stayed on the charts for many weeks — 22 to be exact.

** Eerily, an 'EVERY DAY IS A HOLLY DAY' badge — it was *Buddy Holly Week* around that time — was found in the wreckage.

Life after death

We have already accepted the truth that Buddy Holly and Elvis Presley were both special talents who have gone on to share a similar posthumous fame that shows no sign of dying out.[*] In Holly's case maybe it was something to do with his adopted surname, which via the evergreen holly bush is inextricably linked with Christmas and earlier pagan beliefs, and literally signifies immortality!

It's interesting to reflect that, following his death in 1959, most pundits thought that his fame would be short-lived except for maybe some initial morbid curiosity that might bump-up record sales for a while. Up until the late Fifties, there literally hadn't ever been any 'late, great' musical careers of any significance outside that of Hank Williams, so the thought was that the lives of Holly and his fellow passengers would quickly be forgotten. Indeed, at the time rock & roll itself was still viewed by many as a passing phase.

In any case, death couldn't prolong a career more than fleetingly, for there would only be a finite amount of unreleased material in the vaults, however prolific the artist. And so the rationale of the time went, wasn't it actually rather *unhealthy* to idolise someone who was, well, dead.

Then, as if to demonstrate that for every minus in life a plus seems to pop up, the tears a record company sheds when initially losing one of their artists are probably offset by the silver lining in lower production and marketing costs whilst the remaining material gradually ebbs from their vaults. Inevitably, even if it's a short-lived phenomenon, it's usually at a much quicker rate than before!

This certainly held true in Elvis' case[**], although legalities pertaining to Holly's estate led to his material being eked out over a lengthy period. Despite the release of many commemorative albums and compilations over the years, there are — believe it or not — recordings of his which still await a legal release! Likewise, many of his recordings which originally appeared on vinyl have incredibly still not been issued on compact disc, some two decades after the format was introduced.

The thought which attaches itself to both Elvis and Buddy is that there must be something very special that even now attracts millions of people to them and to their music. Is it in the timbre of Holly's voice, for example, or else the simplicity of the lyrics or the three-chord music he helped to pioneer[***] which have stood the test of time and show no sign of fading away decades later?

What was it that inspired Don McLean to write *American Pie* in the 1970s and, in launching his own career, simultaneously revive that of a long-dead singer with such evocative lyrics? What drove Holly himself to write a

---

[*]   As these words are being written, Elvis is again at the top of the UK singles chart (with *A Little Less Conversation*) — the latest of a small handful of artists to have had posthumous Number Ones. The first, of course, was Buddy Holly, whose poignantly-titled *It Doesn't Matter Anymore* started the trend in April 1959.

[**]   The author recalls RCA running out of Presley product during late 1977 as they strove to keep up with the demand following his death.

[***]   He occasionally humorously introduced numbers on stage during his British tour by saying: 'This is a three-chord song, but the trouble is I can only play two of them!'

song with the ethereal title *Not Fade Away*, having previously inaugurated his career with the statement *That'll Be The Day* and the three words that followed? Were these thoughts being dragged out of his deep subconscious? Was he already doomed to die early? Certainly, Larry Holley has frequently mentioned in interviews that his brother lived his life at such a pace that he must have known he was destined not to live long. Similarly, Elvis was quoted as saying he would not outlive the lifespan of his mother (she died aged forty-six) and in the author's view and those of others such as Larry Geller, he too must somehow have known that his time on earth was limited.

Maybe far in the future when 'vibrations' (for want of a better word) are better understood, we will discover why certain sounds resonate more with some individuals than with others, and in so doing perhaps discover that the rhythm of Buddy Holly's classic composition *Heartbeat* really does somehow chime in with our own heartbeats, or that Presley's heavenly singing really did connect with a higher plane.

As far-fetched as this notion might seem, spiritualists claim that it is precisely because of such vibrations (which make up our etheric being) that you or I sometimes feel an immediate kinship with people we have never met before, or conversely take an irrational dislike to complete strangers for no apparent reason.

And while we're in such a ruminating mood, what inspired Mr. & Mrs. Holley to pen sleeve notes for the 1963 *Reminiscing* album which included such perceptive words as '*Can anyone capture the wind? Has a person ever had a spirit and personality huge enough to encircle the earth? Many may have tried and failed, but we know of one young man who seemed to do these things and far more.*'

Interesting thoughts that were written almost forty years ago and well before anybody could have had any inkling that the music of Buddy Holly would be still with us in the Twenty-First Century. His parents have themselves been gone several years now but would probably have been very proud to know that a 'Buddy Holly Center' would be opened in Lubbock in September 1999, confirming to the world at large that his legacy was here to stay.

As to the strong attraction that Elvis Presley still exhibits, the equation differs only in a matter of degree, as reflected in his acknowledged superstar status. He too has his own museums in the shape of Graceland and the nearby Sun Studios which remain a very focal centre for his fans.

While most of us still remember the huge outpouring of grief at his passing, the raw emotion has subsided to leave behind a career that has continued to blossom despite the fact that neither he or his manager is still around in person. Shameful attempts by some individuals to discredit him after his death actually had the reverse effect, and he is still revered by his many fans throughout the world. Thankfully, the good, positive side of Elvis has vanquished the human frailties which for a time attracted such unhealthy scrutiny. Hopefully the ongoing interest will continue to be positive.

The words of Norman Petty (who's had a pretty poor press since his own death in 1984) recently sprang into my mind. Just hours after the fatal crash, he was interviewed by Snuff Garrett* on KSYD, Wichita Falls, who asked him why the accident had happened. The reply the questioner probably expected was an explanation about the pilot hitting bad weather and perhaps some views on the perils of travelling in light aircraft in wintry conditions. Instead, he received the brief but succinct answer: 'Snuff, we often wonder why things like this do happen, but there's always bound to be a reason somewhere.'

Those seeking a meaning in the deaths of Elvis Presley and Buddy Holly, need look no further than their lives: there is probably no greater consolation than the fact that the wonderful music they made lives on and continues to be handed down to successive generations.

There is a right time for everything

Outside of their own body of work, both Elvis and Buddy have had songs and stories written about them over the years that vouch for the fact that their spirits still move amongst us and are a continuing influence. These range from the documented if heavy thoughts of eighteen different mediums who tried to contact Elvis in the late 1980s, to the more lighthearted fictional work by Bradley Denton, *Buddy Holly Is Alive And Well On Ganymede*, a sci-fi fantasy published in the UK in 1992.

Unfortunately few — if any — fictional stories link Elvis with Buddy Holly, but several years ago, an interesting short story with the innocuous title of *Touring* appeared in a monthly glossy and managed to link up Elvis and Buddy with the unlikely figure of Sixties' legend Janis Joplin. It was a bizarre but well-crafted piece that had the singers sharing a gig in Moorhead, Minnesota in February 1959 — the next venue that Buddy would have appeared at on the *Winter Dance Party* tour had fate not intervened! As the story unfolds, it seems that none of the performers realises that they are in fact dead and they play the show, at the end of which each of them spookily fades away. It makes one wonder whether either Elvis or Buddy, cult figures both, will ever feature in any other works of fiction and, if so, whether they will take on the persona of fictional characters themselves?

Meanwhile, for those readers who are attracted to science fiction, it's a science *fact* that Holly recorded most of his output at the aforesaid Clovis studio just a few miles from the nearest town of Roswell, New Mexico, which is inextricably linked in most people's minds to the subject of alien life forms!** Coincidentally, it was also nearby that Elvis reputedly saw the figure of Christ in the clouds when travelling cross-country, a defining moment for him movingly described by Larry Geller in his book, *If I Can Dream.*

Having taken the reader a long way from Lubbock and Memphis to get this far, I would like to finish with a personal story in the 'believe it or not'

---

* Jerry Allison and Joe B. Mauldin were also interviewed by the deejay, who likewise was a friend of Buddy's. Garrett later produced the 1962 hit album, *Bobby Vee Meets The Crickets.*

** The notorious 'Roswell Incident' concerned the alleged crash-landing of flying saucers in the desert in 1947 quite close to the town. What appeared to be alien bodies and machinery parts from the wrecked craft were quickly spirited away with great speed by the American military, and the matter has been shrouded in secrecy ever since.

category. It unfolded in Clovis, New Mexico during 1996 when my wife and I were visiting the recording studios of Norman Petty, where Holly and the Crickets had recorded most of their classic work. My previous book, *The A–Z Of Buddy Holly*, had come out that very month and I had chosen the cover photo of Buddy at random from literally hundreds that were available and which I had sifted through before rejecting.

These thoughts were far from my mind when Robert Linville, the guide showing us around the studio, suddenly pointed to a particular photo of the singer — one of many that adorned the walls of the small building. He asked me if I knew what was so very special about that particular photograph. Perplexed, I could only politely admit that I had no idea at all of its significance. 'Well,' he explained, 'that's the same photo which we placed in Buddy's casket on the day of his funeral!' Need I add that it was the same one that I had chosen for my book cover? Many would say this is no more than coincidence, but just don't try to convince me that it was anything other than serendipity, because the shiver down my spine is still there.

So where have we reached on our journey? It was a bold step to attempt to establish any sort of link between Elvis Presley and Buddy Holly, but hopefully the reader will agree that the case — to a greater or lesser extent — is proven. For those who don't, I hope that you at least found the discussion stimulating.

Elvis and Buddy, thanks for linking your lives with mine and with so very many others out here. We still dig you!

Glossary

The main text contains many names — some of which will be well known to the reader, many possibly less so — and where appropriate further information is given below by way of a pen-picture. Separate entries have not been raised for all of Elvis' friends and confidantes, but several are mentioned under the 'Memphis Mafia' heading.

ALLISON, Jerry Ivan

Born 1939 in Hill County, near Dallas, Texas and known to all as 'J.I.', drummer Jerry Allison first met Buddy Holly at school in 1952 and joined his group as drummer in 1955. He was to help co-write many of the songs that the Crickets recorded in Clovis, most memorably *That'll Be The Day*. In a rare vocal excursion in 1958, he enjoyed a minor US hit as 'Ivan' with *Real Wild Child* (a Johnny O'Keefe song originally titled *Wild One* that he had brought back with him from an Australian tour). He did try a follow-up single (*Frankie Frankenstein* b/w *That'll Be Alright*), but when that stiffed he went back to his first love of Texas drumming.

When Buddy split from the Crickets in late 1958, it was agreed that Jerry would retain rights to the Crickets name and, although the re-formed group never again scaled the same heights, they did enjoy considerable chart success in the UK during the Sixties, reaching the Top 10 with *Don't Ever Change* and touring there regularly thereafter.

A warm and witty individual, he has since done occasional session work with a host of other artists including Johnny Rivers, the Everly Brothers, Waylon Jennings, Johnny Burnette and Eddie Cochran, as well as playing on the best-selling 1962 album, *Bobby Vee Meets The Crickets*. A major contributor to Buddy Holly's success, he has continued to compose some great material for the Crickets throughout the years up to the present time.

THE BIG BOPPER

The son of an oil worker, Jiles Perry ('Jape') Richardson was born in 1930 in the small oil town of Beaumont, Texas. He spent much of his working life as a deejay on KTRM (the larger-than-life 'Big Bopper') and briefly set a world record in the Fifties when, as a publicity stunt, he played records for 122 hours non-stop on air in a disc-a-thon, which he termed a 'Jape-a-thon'!

Having made a few recordings with little success, he recorded a cash-in called *The Purple People Eater Meets The Witch Doctor* in 1958. When the flip side, *Chantilly Lace*, began getting spins, his singing career well and truly took off. His first major tour, GAC's 1959 *Winter Dance Party*, tragically also proved to be his last when he persuaded Waylon Jennings to give up his seat on the ill-fated plane.

A highly-talented country songwriter, he composed hits for George

Jones, Hank Snow and others, and also discovered Johnny Preston, for whom he penned *Running Bear* and helped perform the background 'grunts'.

He left a wife and two children, his son being born several months after the 1959 plane crash. That son, the Big Bopper Jr, is now a professional entertainer and has recorded his own versions of the dozen or so major songs in his father's legacy.

BLACK, Bill

Born William Patton Black Jr. in 1926, this bassist *par excellence* began his career with Doug Poindexter & The Starlite Wranglers, a small-time country outfit who cut a single for Sun in 1954. Soon after, he and the group's guitarist, Scotty Moore, were recruited by Sam Phillips to back Elvis Presley on his first recordings. They subsequently became his road band, backing him on his early personal appearances across the South during the remainder of 1954 and 1955, and during his first year of national fame, but parted from him in the summer of 1957 following a pay dispute.

Black went on to form the highly successful Bill Black Combo, an instrumental outfit that clocked up an amazing eighteen *Billboard* 'Hot 100' hits and also appeared in the 1961 film, *Teenage Millionaire*, before his untimely death from a brain tumour in 1965. He had also formed his own record and production company, Lyn-Lou, in 1962. He left a wife and three daughters.

BURNETTE, Johnny

Born in 1934, Johnny Burnette was a true contemporary of Elvis Presley. During the Fifties, he lived for a while in the same Memphis housing complex as Elvis, and later also worked for the same electrical company. With his brother Dorsey and guitarist Paul Burlison, he formed the 'Johnny Burnette Rock'n'Roll Trio' and recorded some classic rockabilly tracks for Coral.

Although the cuts were commercially unsuccessful, the brothers found fame shortly afterwards as songwriters for Ricky Nelson with hits like *Waitin' In School*, *Believe What You Say* and *It's Late*, and later as solo artists in the early Sixties. Curiously, although he had five 'Hot 100' chart entries during 1960–61, including big hits with *Dreamin'* and *You're Sixteen,* none of these were self-penned.

Burnette met an untimely end in 1964 when the small, unlit boat he was fishing in was accidentally run down in the twilight by a larger vessel. (Coincidentally the venue of this tragedy was Clear Lake — not the Iowa version as with Holly, but another Clear Lake in California.)

CHARLES, Ray

Born Ray Charles Robinson in 1930 in Albany, Georgia, and completely blind from the age of seven, Brother Ray has to be one of the greatest musical talents of his own or any other time. He first emerged in the early Fifties with recordings very much in the Nat 'King' Cole Trio vein but subsequently went on to carve out a prolific career as a singer/pianist/ songwriter/arranger, even gaining some acting plaudits along the way. His musical output has encompassed most styles of music and many of his most successful records were C&W numbers interpreted in his own inimitable style, although it is with the blues that he remains most closely identified. He was elected to the Rock & Roll Hall Of Fame in its inaugural year (1986) along with both Elvis Presley and Buddy Holly, and was awarded a Grammy *Lifetime Achievement Award* a year later.

We know that Buddy was trying to get in touch with Ray in early 1959 with a view to possibly collaborating on material and it's interesting to reflect that he might actually have become the first of many artists that the blind singer was to work with in the course of his lengthy career.

THE CRICKETS

This entry is not intended as a biographical note, but rather to highlight the difference between the Crickets group of which Buddy Holly was a member and the post-Holly Crickets who recorded from late 1958 onwards.

Following the amicable split with Buddy, the remaining Crickets, Jerry Allison and Joe B. Mauldin, drafted in vocalist Earl Sinks and returned to the Lubbock area to work with Norman Petty. They went on to carve out a long career, albeit with several changes of style and personnel along the way.

At the time of writing, Buddy's friend and fellow-musician Sonny Curtis is lead vocalist and the group stay largely faithful to the Holly songbook, augmenting it with material from the latter's prolific pen. It's sobering to think that they have been together longer even than the Rolling Stones. Jerry, Sonny and Joe B. now all live close to Nashville, Tennessee, where they also own their own recording facility — the Branch Studio — situated on Jerry's farm in Lyles, Tennessee.

CURTIS, Sonny

Born 1937 in Meadow, Texas, close to Lubbock, Sonny Curtis is a talented singer/songwriter with a highly impressive musical pedigree that includes playing guitar with Buddy Holly as a teenager in the Fifties, co-writing *Rock Around With Ollie Vee* (probably the best rockabilly-styled number that Holly ever recorded) and fronting the Crickets through into the new millennium.

In between, he has enjoyed a diverse career as a musician and composer, penning *Walk Right Back* for the Everly Brothers and *I Fought The Law* for the Bobby Fuller Four, and co-writing *More Than I Can Say* (a hit for Bobby Vee in 1961 and Leo Sayer in 1980) with Cricket Jerry Allison. He also co-wrote Keith Whitley's *I'm No Stranger To The Rain* (a No. 1 C&W single in the USA in 1989) with Ron Hellard. He has decidedly firm views about the way Buddy Holly's life and career have both been misrepresented over the years and corrected a few myths with his excellent 1980 recording, *The Real Buddy Holly Story*.

DARIN, Bobby

This multi-talented individual born Walden Robert Cassotto in New York in 1936 is commonly listed as a vocalist/guitarist/pianist/drummer in rock obituaries. Saddled with heart problems as a result of contracting rheumatic fever as a child, he was always racing against time as he was not expected survive into adulthood. He went on to have a continuous fifteen-year run of hits in the USA which started in 1958 and only finished the year he died aged just thirty-seven.

Darin's music ranged from rock & roll to standards to folk to country, and he refused to limit himself to any one style. In fact, he'd just signed with Motown before his death in 1973. He was elected to the Rock & Roll Hall Of Fame in 1990. He married twice — most prominently to actress Sandra Dee by whom he had a son, Todd.

GELLER, Larry

Born in 1940, Larry Geller was a hairdresser at the Beverly Hills salon of Jay Sebring, a flamboyant individual who sadly was one of several victims of the notorious murderer, Charles Manson. He was introduced to Elvis in 1964 and became his personal hairdresser until pushed out in the spring of 1967 by Colonel Parker. He subsequently returned in late 1972 and remained with him for the rest of his life.

It was Geller who introduced Elvis to the 'mystical', a word used here to encompass religion, spirituality and parapsychology. Presley always referred to him as his friend and guru, and there was a close bond between them until the end.

Geller co-wrote the 1989 book, *If I Can Dream*, with Joel Spector, and in 1998 collaborated with author Jess Stearn on another, *Elvis' Search For God*. He remains in the hair care business and has also launched his own product line.

GUESS, Don

Born 1937 in Aspermont, Texas, Don Guess played bass with Buddy Holly in the early days and was on all three of his 1956 Decca sessions in Nashville. It is thought that it was Guess (who had lived for some time in New Mexico) that first drew Holly's attention to Norman Petty's studio in Clovis.

In later years, Guess made a few solo recordings for regional labels and also had a release on Brunswick in the Fifties which never charted. Always on the fringe of the record scene, he later established his own insurance business in El Paso. He died in 1992 of cancer.

HARDIN, Glen D.

A name that neatly links that of Buddy Holly with Elvis Presley, Glen Hardin was born in Collingsworth County near Lubbock in 1939, although he spent much of his childhood in Oklahoma. The son of a cowboy, he went on to become a talented keyboard player and, although he knew Buddy, he was never a member of his original group. He did, however, join the Crickets in the early Sixties and wrote much of their material.

Later on, he worked with Elvis from 1970 to 1976 as pianist and arranger, and can often be glimpsed in film footage of the singer's Seventies' concerts.

In recent times, he has occasionally toured and recorded with the Crickets, but has also had some heart trouble which has curtailed his activities.

HOLLEY family

Buddy's parents are both deceased but lived on into their eighties, while his brothers Larry and Travis and sister Pat are still alive and well and living in and around Lubbock. The Holley Tile Company still operates as it has for many years, and these days Buddy's niece, Sherry, helps to run it.

HOLLY, Maria Elena

Buddy met Maria Elena Santiago at Southern Music in New York in January 1958, and the couple were married in Lubbock on 15 August that same year. At the time of the February 1959 plane crash, Maria Elena was pregnant and tragically lost the baby she was carrying as a result of the shock.

She later remarried (and subsequently divorced) having three children along the way and now lives in Dallas, from where she zealously guards the posthumous career of her late husband. Forty years on, there is still a lawsuit outstanding against MCA (who now own the rights to his Decca, Coral and Brunswick recordings), which she and others are pursuing.

It is extremely disappointing that, in trying to protect her husband's image and memory, she sometimes appears to act against the interests of *bona fide* fans by delaying the legal release of Holly material that has been in unofficial circulation for years.

JARVIS, Felton

As a record producer, Felton Jarvis worked with a whole range of famous names, but he is probably best-remembered for his work with Elvis Presley at RCA. He is also due credit for helping to stop the King's career from going completely downhill in the Seventies by encouraging him to tackle more challenging material. By this time, he had left RCA and was working for Elvis as a freelance. He went on to overdub some of Presley's material after his death in 1977, but died himself in 1981 as the result of a stroke following a long battle with ill-health. He was only 45 years old.

JENNINGS, Waylon

Born 1937 in Littlefield, Texas, Jennings first got to know Buddy Holly in the early Fifties when the latter began appearing regularly on KDAV's *Sunday Party*. Thereafter, he became a disc jockey himself for another local station, KLLL, where Buddy would often stop by to see him after he'd hit the big time.

Co-opted by Buddy to play bass for him on the 1959 *Winter Dance Party* tour, Jennings famously gave up his place on the ill-fated plane to the Big Bopper, who had flu. He later wrote an autobiography, *Waylon*, cataloguing his days with Holly, whom he regarded as his mentor.

Jennings went on to carve out a huge country music career in the Seventies, achieving notoriety as 'the Nashville Rebel' and was elected to the Country Music Hall Of Fame in 2001. Sadly, his later years were blighted by a lengthy battle with drugs, and the diabetes-related problems to which he finally succumbed in February 2002 aged 64.

LEIBER & STOLLER

One of the greatest songwriting teams of the rock & roll era, Jerry Leiber and Mike Stoller — both born in 1933 — first collaborated in 1949, writing several hits in the rhythm & blues idiom. In the mid-Fifties, they found immense success with compositions for the Coasters and the Drifters, as a result of which they were engaged to write material for Elvis. They penned the title songs (and others) for his *Loving You*, *Jailhouse Rock* and *King Creole* movies, but were dropped thereafter — much to Presley's dismay. Their songwriting talents were recently celebrated in the stage musical *Smokey Joe's Cafe*, the title of one of their songs (and, incidentally, one of only two Leiber–Stoller songs that Buddy Holly recorded, the other being *Baby I Don't Care*).

MAULDIN, Joe B.

Born 1940 in Lubbock, Joseph Benson Mauldin Jr. was the youngest of the Crickets, although he briefly played stand-up bass with Terry Noland's group, the Four Teens, before meeting up with Holly. As with Jerry Allison, he parted company with Buddy in late 1958 and actually left the music business for a year or so in the early Sixties. He later worked as a recording engineer with Snuff Garrett in Los Angeles and at the famous Gold Star studios, and was also the West Coast agent for George Pincus Music, before rejoining the re-formed Crickets, with whom he has remained to the present day.

MEMPHIS MAFIA

This was the disparaging name used to describe the posse of individuals with whom Elvis surrounded himself after his return from the army. They were in fact 'taking care of business' — hence the TCB logo — and were mostly friends that became employees or members of his 'corporation', to use the term Elvis favoured. More than twenty names will be familiar to most fans of the King, but a few must be singled out for special mention.

Charlie Hodge was there from the time he and Elvis first met in 1956 until the early hours of 16 August 1977, when he helped transport the singer's lifeless body to the hospital. Much more than just a friend, Hodge was both a musician and vocalist himself who over the years became indispensable to Elvis.

Red West and his cousin **Sonny West** had been friends of Elvis since his Memphis schooldays and were his favoured bodyguards until shortly before his death. Leaving under a cloud, they went on to write an exposé of the singer with fellow minder **Dave Hebler** called *Elvis: What Happened?* Published just days before Presley's death, it can be read either as a belated warning to their former employer or a sensationalised account of his life.

Joe Esposito, **Lamar Fike**, **Alan Fortas**, **Marty Lacker** and **Jerry Schilling** were also main players, as was Elvis' step-brother **David Stanley**, who went on to write *Elvis, We Love You Tender* and also compiled an encyclopaedia about the singer.

Last but not least, there was also Elvis' spiritual mentor, **Larry Geller**, who is the subject of a separate entry above.

MONTGOMERY, Bob

Born in 1937 in Lampasas, Texas, Bob Montgomery became firm friends with Buddy Holly at school and formed the Buddy & Bob duo with him in 1954. The two were inseparable during that time and together they wrote several classic compositions, the best of which was *Heartbeat*.

After Buddy got the break that took him to Nashville in early 1956, he went to work at Norman Petty's Clovis studio as an engineer and also made a few recordings himself before moving to Nashville in the mid-Sixties. There, he went on to carve out a respectable career in country music, forming the House Of Gold music publishing business and producing hits for the likes of Bobby Goldsboro and Janie Fricke.

Bob retired a few years ago and returned to the Lubbock area. His son Kevin now works in the music business and contributed *Wishing* (a duet with Mary Chapin Carpenter) to the 1996 Nashville Holly tribute album, *Not Fade Away*. In a recent televised documentary about Holly's life, he recalled with affection how he, Buddy and Elvis all went to the movies together when the latter first came to Lubbock.

MOORE, Scotty

Born Winfield Scott Moore III in December 1931, Scotty is alive and well having now reached the venerable age of 70. His earliest incarnation was as lead guitarist with Doug Poindexter & The Starlite Wranglers, a small-time country outfit who cut a single for Sun in 1954. Soon after, he and the group's bassist, Bill Black, were recruited by Sam Phillips to back Elvis Presley on his first recordings. They subsequently became his road band, backing him on his early personal appearances across the South. During the second half of 1954, Moore also acted as Presley's manager, passing the reins over to Bob Neal in January 1955.

Scotty and Bill parted company with Elvis in 1957 following a pay dispute. Bill never came back, but Scotty did return for a prolonged spell from

1960–68, famously putting in a final appearance on the NBC-TV *Elvis* 'comeback special in December 1968.

He later moved into radio work as an engineer, cut an album with Ral Donner, and in 1994 recorded the critically-acclaimed album, *The Guitar That Changed The World*. He also got to tell his version of life with his former boss in *That's Alright, Elvis: The Untold Story Of Elvis's First Guitarist And Manager, Scotty Moore.*

NEAL, Bob

Bob Neal was born in 1917 in the Belgian Congo and arrived in the USA during 1930. He was a music agent and disc jockey in Memphis before turning to full-time management, handling Elvis' career for the fifteen months from January 1955 to April 1956, when he had to give way to the thrusting Colonel Tom Parker. He did, however, go on to manage the remainder of the 'Million Dollar Quartet' — Jerry Lee Lewis, Johnny Cash and Carl Perkins — and a host of other Southern stars.

ORBISON, Roy

The legendary singer/songwriter who will forever be known as 'the Big O' was born in 1936 in Vernon, Texas. He made his first recordings with Norman Petty at Clovis before moving to Sun, where he achieved some modest in 1956 with his own composition, *Ooby Dooby*. National and international success finally arrived in 1960 with a succession of self-penned big ballads including *Only The Lonely*, *Running Scared*, *Crying* and *Oh, Pretty Woman.*

Although there were some lulls in his later career, he was beginning to achieve renewed success in the Eighties with the Traveling Wilburys when he succumbed to a heart attack in 1988 at the age of just 52. In 1989, Ellis Amburn (author of *The Real Buddy Holly Story* and a book on fellow Texan Janis Joplin) penned what is for the moment probably the definitive biography of the singer, *Dark Star.*

PARKER, Colonel Tom

Born Andreas Cornelius van Kuijk in Holland in 1909, Elvis Presley's famous (or should that be *in*famous?) manager is stripped of his honorary title of 'Colonel' for the duration of this entry! Through his Jamboree Attractions, Parker had managed country legends Eddy Arnold and Hank Snow before Elvis became his one and only client in 1965, literally 'till death us do part'.

US movie and gossip columnist May Mann (no relation to the author), wrote a biography of the relationship between manager and singer, *Elvis And The Colonel*, but this was back in 1975 when the law of libel would have been somewhat inhibiting as both parties were still alive. Since that time, much more information has been revealed into the background of Parker and most of this does not cast him in a very favourable light. Having spent most of his declining years at the gaming tables in Vegas, he died in 1997 at the age of 87 from complications following a stroke.

PETTY, Norman

Born in 1927 in Clovis, New Mexico, Norman Petty set up an independent recording studio in his home town in 1955, and this was where Buddy Holly and the Crickets recorded the bulk of their hits. Petty was also a fine keyboard player and led his own easy-listening group, the Norman Petty Trio, for several years. In fact, their first hit, 1954's *Mood Indigo*, helped to finance the building of the studio. In 1957, *Almost Paradise* and *The First Kiss* both made the *Billboard* 'Top 100'.

In the Fifties, other local talents including Roy Orbison, Buddy Knox and Jimmy Bowen also recorded at Clovis. After Holly's death, Petty continued to be involved with hit acts including the Bobby Fuller Four, the String-A-Longs and the Fireballs (whom he also used to overdub most of Holly's posthumous releases during the Sixties).

A talented musician and producer, Petty died in 1984 of leukaemia.

PHILLIPS, Dewey

Born in 1926, Phillips was a high-energy Memphis disc jockey famed for his wild *Red Hot & Blue* show which debuted on WHBQ in 1948. Although he was no relation to Sam Phillips, both men championed the same kind of music — R&B. They formed a short-lived record company together (The Phillips) in 1950 and continued to help each another over the years. For example, Phillips helped to put Elvis Presley's name on the map by playing *That's All Right (Mama)* fourteen times in the course of one programme! He later began to behave erratically after developing a drink problem and died prematurely in 1968 at the same age as Elvis (42).

PHILLIPS, Sam

Born 1923 in Alabama, Sam Cornelius Phillips was still a relatively young man when Elvis first wandered into the Sun studios at 706 Union Avenue that fateful day in 1953. He had been a disc jockey at various radio stations before setting up the Memphis Recording Service in 1950 and producing some seminal R&B recordings by the likes of Jackie Brenston, B.B. King and Howlin' Wolf.

In 1952, he founded his own label, Sun, and soon began turning his energies to a procession of white hopefuls with an exciting new sound rooted both in R&B and country music. Among the other great names associated with Phillips in the Fifties were Johnny Cash, Carl Perkins, Roy Orbison and Jerry Lee Lewis as well as lesser-known but equally revered rockabilly performers like Billy Lee Riley, Warren Smith, Sonny Burgess and Charlie Feathers.

THE PICKS

The Picks were a vocal trio from the Lubbock area consisting of brothers Bill and John Pickering and Bob Lapham. Norman Petty often used them to provide backing vocals for many artists at his Clovis studios.

Probably the most famous sessions on which they appeared were those in 1957 for a batch of Buddy Holly recordings that ended up on the *Chirping Crickets* album including *Maybe Baby* and *Tell Me How*. The group's vocals were usually overdubbed after the vocal and instrumental tracks had been completed.

In the Eighties, just before Bill Pickering died, they went into a Houston studio and overdubbed backing vocals on many other Holly recordings with somewhat mixed results.

PRESLEY, Lisa Marie

Born in 1968, Lisa Marie is the only child of Elvis and Priscilla Presley. She is the sole heir to the estate of the singer and, happily for his fans, has decided to keep Graceland open to the public for the foreseeable future. It remains one of the most visited sites in the world.

She has two children from her first marriage and was, somewhat bizarrely, married to the singer Michael Jackson for a brief period. At the present time, it is rumoured that she is belatedly contemplating a career in music. It is said that she is a member of the Church of Scientology, the sect founded in 1952 by L. Ron Hubbard, and which ten years ago was listed as having a worldwide membership of over seven million.

PRESLEY, Priscilla

The only wife of Elvis Presley, Priscilla was born in 1945 and was adopted by Joseph Beaulieu after her father was killed in a plane crash. She first met Elvis in 1959 when he and her step-father were both stationed with the army in West Germany. Their courtship was rather unconventional given that Priscilla was just fourteen years old at the outset, but she went to live at Graceland from 1960 onwards and completed her schooling in Memphis. The couple finally married in 1967 and their only daughter, Lisa Marie, came along exactly nine months later.

Elvis and Priscilla separated in 1972 and their divorce was finalised late the following year. In 1985, the former Mrs. Presley wrote *Elvis And Me*, a straightforward if rather bland account of their life together. She later became an actress with high-profile roles in the hit TV soap *Dallas* and the highly amusing *Naked Gun* movies.

She acted as the trustee of Elvis' former home at Graceland until 1993, when their daughter Lisa Marie — the sole heir to the singer's estate — finally reached the age of 25. She has never remarried.

PRESLEY, Vernon and Gladys

Elvis' parents were both born in rural Mississippi in the early 1900s. Married in 1933, they stayed together until separated by Gladys' untimely death from acute hepatitis in 1958 at the age of forty-six (not forty-two as is often stated). Happily, she lived long enough to witness the early impact her son had on the music and film world. (As a note of trivia, both parents can be clearly seen in the audience while Elvis sings several numbers in the film *Loving You*.)

Vernon went on to marry Dee Stanley and became step-father to her three sons, but the marriage ended in divorce. He later developed heart problems, from which he died in 1979 at the age of 63.

THE ROSES

In addition to the Picks, Norman Petty also engaged the Roses (Robert Linville, David Bigham and Ray Rush) to provide backing vocals for several 1958 Crickets recordings including *Think It Over* and *It's So Easy*. They also toured with the Crickets that year, backing them on stage on the *Biggest Show Of Stars For 1958* extravaganza — the one and only time this happened. They also made several recordings in their own right during the Fifties for the Dot label.

A mainstay for years of the *Annual Music Festival* in Clovis, Robert Linville sadly died in late 2001 at the age of 65 after losing his fight against cancer. Any of the frequent visitors to the old Clovis studios in recent years would invariably have been shown around by him and will remember his warmth and unfailing hospitality.

SULLIVAN, Niki

A third cousin of Buddy Holly (although neither of them realised it when they first met), Niki Sullivan was born in 1937 in South Gate, California and moved to Lubbock a few years later. He met Buddy around 1956 and was the Crickets' rhythm guitarist for most of 1957. He tried his luck as a solo artist on Dot in 1958, then fronting several groups including the Plainsmen and the Hollyhawks (the latter managed by Buddy's father, L.O. Holley), but failed to make any real impact and eventually quit music to work for the Sony organisation, with whom he has remained ever since. He briefly came out of musical retirement in 1999 to take part in the *40th Anniversary Winter Dance Party* tour.

VALENS, Ritchie

Born Richard Steven Valenzuela in a poor district of Los Angeles in 1941, Valens literally went from rags to riches when his first Del-Fi release, *Come On, Let's Go*, became a US Top 50 hit in the autumn of 1958. His second single, *Donna* b/w *La Bamba*, rocketed to No. 2 in the *Billboard* 'Hot 100' over the year end and he was quickly booked onto the *Winter Dance Party* tour.

Although only seventeen, Valens was a promising singer/guitarist/songwriter who had already appeared in his first rock & roll movie, *Go, Johnny, Go*. In 1978, another film — *La Bamba*, an evocative portrait of his life starring Lee Diamond Phillips — renewed interest in his work. He was belatedly elected to the Rock & Roll Hall Of Fame in 2001.

WALKER, Billy

Born 1929 in Texas, Billy Walker enjoyed a lengthy career in country music with over fifty C&W chart hits to his name. In 1960, he even briefly crossed over into the pop charts with *Forever*.

In earlier times, Walker had worked as a deejay in Clovis, New Mexico — which is where he got to meet Norman Petty — and recorded there on occasion during the Fifties. In particular, he cut a couple of tracks there in 1957 when the Crickets were in the studio working on *Words Of Love* and a couple of other songs. There is a strong possibility that Holly played guitar on Walker's recordings, *On My Mind Again* and *Viva La Matador* (Columbia), although Walker himself has alternately confirmed and then denied this fact!

WELBORN, Larry

Born 1939 in Oklahoma, Larry Welborn moved to Lubbock as a teenager and played bass with Buddy Holly and Bob Montgomery ('Buddy & Bob') before joining Terry Noland's Four Teens as guitarist in 1956. He appeared on several early Holly demos including *Bo Diddley* and *Brown Eyed Handsome Man*, as well as the hit version of *That'll Be The Day*. While he failed to make any money for playing on the session that produced the latter track, he did belatedly receive a gold disc for it in 1986. The fact that the special presentation was made by Paul McCartney went some way to make up for the earlier oversight. In later years, Larry returned to his native Oklahoma.

Larry Welborn was one of only a trio of bassists to record with Holly at Clovis, the others being Joe B. Mauldin and the oft-overlooked George Atwood, who was frequently used by Norman Petty as a house musician and sat in when needed. Amongst the handful of classic recordings he was to make with Buddy were *Heartbeat* and *Love's Made A Fool Of You*.

Bibliography

The printed word concerning Elvis is overwhelming and like Topsy is still growing, so for this reason if no other any bibliography must be selective in nature. In contrast, the number of books (and some excellent booklets) on Buddy Holly is smaller but expanding, after a slow start that didn't see the first full-scale biography until the 1970s when John Goldrosen set the wheels in motion. What follows in the bibliography listed below predominantly relates specifically to these two great artists.

However, the names of many other singers and songwriters from that golden era are also scattered throughout the course of this work, and it has therefore been necessary to consult a great many other books, magazines and periodicals along the way. The author has been a fan of the music since first it burst upon us in the Fifties and has a library of several hundred books to call upon but nevertheless, as others have said before, every article, book and sleevenote read in the course of a long life may well have helped.

In restricting the list to only fifty or so books, many excellent works such as the series of publications on Elvis by Ger Rijff have been omitted, whilst other less deserving books may have been included. But in mitigation the reader will observe that room has not been found to list any of Albert Goldman's biographies!

The Guinness *British Hit Singles* and *British Hit Albums* books have been essential reading, and were supplemented in the last year by a volume from Music Mentor Books covering the much-neglected EP charts. Also, the series of *Rock Family Trees* books by Pete Frame — each volume a veritable work of art — have been of help, as have the compilations of the US *Billboard* charts published by Joel Whitburn.

Finally, the *Guinness Who's Who Of* series edited by Colin Larkin (recently revised and republished by Virgin) has been an extremely useful source of reference.

BOOKS

Amburn, Ellis - *Dark Star* (Hodder & Stoughton, London) 1989   *[Roy Orbison biography]*
Amburn, Ellis - *The Real Buddy Holly Story* (Virgin, London) 1996
Anderson, Robert, & Gail North - *Gospel Music Encyclopedia* (Sterling, New York) 1979
Bacon, Tony, & Paul Day - *The Fender Book* (Balafon, New York) 1992
Bleasdale, Alan - *Are You Lonesome Tonight?* (Faber & Faber) 1985   *[play]*
Bowen, Jimmy, & Jim Jerome - *Rough Mix* (Simon & Schuster, New York) 1997
Burk, Bill E. - *Early Elvis — The Tupelo Years* (Propwash, Memphis) 1994
Clayson, Alan - *Death Discs* (Gollancz, London) 1993
Claton, Rose, & Dick Heard - *Elvis — In The Words Of Those Who Knew Him Best*
                              (Virgin, London) 1994
Cotten, Lee - *Did Elvis Sing In Your Hometown?* (High Sierra, Sacramento, CA) 1995
Cotten, Lee - *Did Elvis Sing In Your Hometown Too?* (High Sierra, Sacramento, CA) 1997
Dawson, Jim, & Spencer Leigh - *Memories Of Buddy Holly* (Big Nickel, Milford, NH) 1996
Dawson, Jim, & Steve Propes - *What Was The First Rock & Roll Record?*
                              (Faber & Faber, London) 1992
DiOrio, Al - *Borrowed Time* (Running Press, Philadelphia) 1986   *[Bobby Darin biography]*
Dundy, Elaine - *Elvis And Gladys* (Macmillan, New York) 1985
Escott, Colin, with Martin Hawkins - *Good Rockin' Tonight* (St. Martin's Press, New York) 1991
Farren, Mick - *Elvis In His Own Words* (Omnibus, London) 1977
Geller, Larry, & Joel Spector - *If I Can Dream* (Century, London) 1989

Gillett, Charlie - *The Sound Of The City* (Sphere, London) 1971
Goldrosen, John - *Buddy Holly: His Life And Music* (Quick Fox, New York) 1979
Goldrosen, John, & John Beecher - *Remembering Buddy* (Omnibus, London) 1996
Goldschneider, Gary, & Joost Elffers - *The Secret Language Of Relationships*
(Shaftesbury) 1998
Guralnick, Peter - *Last Train To Memphis* (Little, Brown, London) 1995
Guralnick, Peter - *Careless Love* (Little Brown, London) 1999
Hardy, Phil, & Dave Laing - *Faber Companion To 20th Century Popular Music*
(Faber & Faber, London) 1990
Hazen, Cindy, & Mike Freeman - *The Best Of Elvis: Recollections Of A Great Humanitarian*
(Memphis Explorations, Memphis) 1992
Jackson, John A. - *Big Beat Heat* (Schirmer, New York) 1991 *[Alan Freed biography]*
Jennings, Waylon, with Lenny Kaye - *Waylon* (Warner, New York) 1996
Jorgensen, Ernst - *Elvis Presley: A Life In Music* (St. Martin's Press, New York) 1998
Juanico, June - *Elvis In The Twilight Of Memory* (Little Brown, London) 1997
Knight, Tim - *Chantilly Lace* (Port Arthur Historical Society, Port Arthur, TX) 1989
[Big Bopper biography]
Koster, Nick - *Texas Music* (St. Martin's Griffin, New York) 2000
Lehmer, Larry - *The Day The Music Died* (Schirmer, New York) 1997
Mann, Alan - *The A To Z Of Buddy Holly* (Aurum, London) 1996
Marcus, Greil - *Dead Elvis* (Viking, London) 1991
Mendheim, Beverly - *Ritchie Valens: The First Latino Rocker* (Bilingual Press, Tempe, AZ) 1987
Mundy, Julie, & Darrel Higham - *Don't Forget Me* (Mainstream, Edinburgh) 2000
[Eddie Cochran biography]
Repsch, John - *The Legendary Joe Meek* (Woodford House, London) 1989
Robinson, Red, & Peggy Hodgins - *Rockbound* (Hancock House, Surrey, BC, Canada) 1983
Schroer, Andreas - *Private Presley* (William Morrow, New York) 1993
Scott, Frank, & Al Ennis - *The Roots & Rhythm Guide To Rock* (A Capella, Chicago) 1993
Silverton, Peter - *Essential Elvis* (Chameleon, London) 1997
Stearn, Jess - *Elvis' Search For God* (Greenleaf, Murfreesboro, TN) 1998
Talevski, Nick - *Tombstone Blues: Encyclopaedia Of Rock Obituaries* (Omnibus, London) 1999
Thiele, Bob - *What A Wonderful World* (Oxford University Press, New York) 1995
Various - *The Rolling Stone Illustrated History Of Rock & Roll* (Plexus, London) 1992
Various - *The Ultimate Beatles Encyclopaedia* (Virgin, London) 1992
Warner, Alan - *Who Sang What In Rock'n'Roll?* (Blandford, London) 1990
West, Red & Sonny, with Dave Hebler - *Elvis: What Happened?* (William Collins) 1997
Worth, Fred L., & Steve Temerius - *Elvis: His Life From A To Z* (Corgi) 1989

BOOKLETS & PERIODICALS

Buddy Holly Day-By-Day [USA]   Series of five booklets by Bill Griggs, published in 1997.
Crickets File [UK]   Quarterly magazine (edited by John Firminger)
Elvis -The Man And His Music [UK]   Quarterly sister publication to *Now Dig This* (below).
History Of Rock [UK]   10-volume partwork published by Orbis 1982–84.
Holly International [UK]   Quarterly magazine (edited by Jim Carr).
Now Dig This [UK]   The UK's leading rock & roll magazine (edited by Trevor Cajiao).
Various publications - Alan Clark
Various publications - John Ingman

Index

ILLUSTRATIONS AND PHOTO CREDITS

Ads on pages 69, 74 and 84 courtesy of Alan Clark; ad on page 73 courtesy of Lubbock Avalanche-Journal and John Beecher/Rollercoaster Records; ad on page 81 courtesy of Lubbock Avalanche-Journal/Chris Rees; ad on page 97 courtesy of Alan Clark/Chris Rees.

Photo on page 24 by unknown photographer (Courtesy of Colin Escott/Showtime Archives); photo on page 27 by Langston McEachern (Courtesy of Colin Escott); photo on page 28 by unknown photographer (Courtesy of Don Guess/Derek Glenister); photo on page 29 by Rallo Henry (Courtesy of Bill Griggs/BHMS); photo on page 31 by unknown photographer (Courtesy of Larry Holley/Chris Rees); photo on page 37 by Steve Cairns (Courtesy of Steve Cairns); photos on pages 38, 79, 113, 115 and 117 by unknown photographers (Courtesy of Trevor Cajiao/Now Dig This); photos on pages 42 and 43 by unknown photographers (Courtesy of Steve Cairns); photo on page 48 by John Goldrosen (Courtesy of John Beecher/Rollercoaster Records and Chris Rees); photos on pages 49 and 50 by unknown photographers (Courtesy of Holley family/Chris Rees); photos on pages 56, 57, 58, 59, 60, 80 and 121 by unknown photographers (Courtesy of George R. White); James Dean photo on page 62 by unknown photographer (Courtesy Warner Bros/George R. White); Elvis photo on page 62 by unknown photographer (Courtesy of John Beecher/Rollercoaster Records); photo on page 66 by unknown photographer (Courtesy of Dave Stone/Chris Rees); photo on page 71 by unknown photographer (Courtesy of Steve Bonner via Bill Griggs/BHMS); photos on pages 82 and 83 by unknown photographer (Courtesy of Bill Griggs/BHMS); photo on page 85 by Ben Hall (Courtesy of John Beecher/Rollercoaster Records); photo on page 91 by unknown photographer (Courtesy of Prairie Dog/Chris Rees); photo on page 92 by unknown photographer (Courtesy of Decca Records/Chris Rees); photo on page 94 by unknown photographer (Courtesy of Chris Rees); photo on page 96 by June Clark (Courtesy of Chris Rees); photo on page 99 by Jerry Zapata (Courtesy of John Beecher/Rollercoaster Records); photo on page 100 by unknown photographer (Courtesy of Jerry Zapata); photo on page 102 copyright Lew Allen, TM/CMG Worldwide & Maria Elena Holly (Courtesy of Lew Allen); photo on page 116 by unknown photographer (Courtesy of Johnny Vallis); photo on page 119 by unknown photographer (Courtesy of M-G-M and Trevor Cajiao/Now Dig This).

OTHER TITLES FROM MUSIC MENTOR BOOKS

The Complete Bo Diddley Sessions
George R. White
ISBN 0-9519888-0-8 *(paperback, 92 pages)* **1993**

Complete US/UK discography of this legendary American guitarist by the man who knows him best — his biographer. Includes band history, session details, list of all US/UK releases from 1955 to 1992, selected foreign rarities, BBC radio recordings, film and video performances, guest appearances on other artists' sessions, label shots, vintage ads, etc.

(35 Years of) British Hit EPs
George R. White
ISBN 0-9519888-1-6 *(paperback, 256 pages)* **2001**

At last, a chart book dedicated to British hit EPs! Includes a history of the format, an artist-by-artist listing of every 7-inch EP hit from 1955 to 1989 (with full track details for each record), analyses of chart performance, and — for the first time ever — the official UK EP charts reproduced in their entirety. Profusely illustrated with *over 600* sleeve shots. A collector's dream!

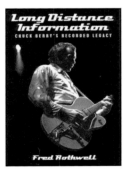

Long Distance Information: Chuck Berry's Recorded Legacy
Fred Rothwell
ISBN 0-9519888-2-4 *(paperback, 352 pages)* **2001**

Detailed analysis of every recording Chuck Berry has ever made. Includes an overview of his life and career, his influences, the stories behind his most famous compositions, full session details, listings of all his key US/UK vinyl and CD releases (including track details), TV and film appearances, and much, much more. Over 100 illustrations including label shots, vintage ads and previously unpublished photos.

On The Road
Dave Nicolson
ISBN 0-9519888-4-0 *(paperback, 256 pages)* **2002**

Gary 'US' Bonds, Pat Boone, Freddy Cannon, Crickets Jerry Allison, Sonny Curtis and Joe B. Mauldin, Bo Diddley, Dion, Fats Domino, Duane Eddy, Frankie Ford, Charlie Gracie, Brian Hyland, Marv Johnson, Ben E. King, Brenda Lee, Little Eva, Chris Montez, Johnny Moore (Drifters), Gene Pitney, Johnny Preston, Tommy Roe, Del Shannon, Edwin Starr, Johnny Tillotson and Bobby Vee tell the fascinating stories of their careers as hitmakers and beyond. Over 150 illustrations.

**Music Mentor books
are available from all good bookshops
or by mail order from:**

Music Mentor Books
69 Station Road
Upper Poppleton
YORK YO26 6PZ
England

Telephone/Fax: 01904 330308
International Telephone/Fax: +44 1904 330308
email: music.mentor@lineone.net
website: http://musicmentor0.tripod.com